DIVERSIFICATION AND SUSTAINABLE RURAL LIVELIHOOD

About the Authors

H.S. Shylendra is a faculty at Institute of Rural Management, Anand (IRMA). He did his Ph.D. in Economics from Institute for Social and Economic Change, Bangalore. His areas of interest are sustainable rural development, rural livelihood systems, micro/rural finance, and governance. Currently, he teaches courses on Rural Development and Micro-Finance for the students of the Post-Graduate Programme at IRMA. He has co-authored two monographs, titled *Organising for Rural Development* and *Sustainable Livelihood in the Context of Growing Occupational Diversification and Rural-Urban Linkages.* Also, he has some research papers to his credit.

Uma Rani is a faculty at Gujarat Institute of Development Research (GIDR), Ahmedabad. She holds a Ph.D. degree in Economics from the University of Hyderabad. She specialises in the area of Labour Economics. Currently, she is pursuing research on the employment potential of the informal sector.

DIVERSIFICATION AND SUSTAINABLE RURAL LIVELIHOOD

(A Study in the Semi-Arid Villages of Western India)

H.S. Shylendra
Uma Rani

CONCEPT PUBLISHING COMPANY, NEW DELHI-110059

Cataloging in Publication Data—DK
Courtesy: D.K. Agencies (P) Ltd. <docinfo@dkagencies.com>

Shylendra, H. S.
Diversification and sustainable rural livelihood : a study in the semi-arid villages of western India / H.S. Shylendra, Uma Rani.
p. cm.
Includes bibliographical references (p.)
Includes index.
ISBN 8180692051

1. Migrant labor—India—Gujarat. 2. Rural-urban migration—India—Gujarat. 3. Rural development—India—Gujarat. 4. Sustainable development—India—Gujarat. I. Uma Rani, joint author. II. Title.

DDC 331.544 095 475 21

ISBN 81-8069-205-1

First Published 2005

Published and Printed by
Ashok Kumar Mittal
Concept Publishing Company
A/15-16, Commercial Block, Mohan Garden,
New Delhi-110 059 (India)

Phones : 25351460, 25351794
Fas : +91-11-25357103
Email : publishing@conceptpub.com

PREFACE AND ACKNOWLEDGEMENTS

The present book is an outcome of a two-phase Indo-Swiss collaborative research project carried out during 1994-2000 at the Institute of Rural Management, Anand. The project funded by Swiss National Science Foundation (SNSF) through NADEL of Federal Institute of Technology, Zurich, Switzerland had been initiated primarily with the intention of helping the Swiss Agency for Development Co-operation (SDC) to formulate its sector strategy for sustainable land use in semi-arid areas in India. Given the complex nature of the concept of sustainability, the research team involved had decided at the very beginning to examine the concept more holistically rather take any narrow view. The first phase of the project was meant to identify through an exploratory research all the major and relevant themes having a bearing on the concept of livelihood sustainability. The theme of the present book, occupational diversification, came to be identified by the team in the course of the exploratory research of the first phase.

It will also be interesting here to share how exactly the theme came to be selected and how we got convinced of its relevance for addressing the issue of rural livelihood security and sustainability. When the first author visited village Mahudi, one of the three study villages, for the first time during the summer of 1994, he encountered a peculiar situation. During the visit, though the village had over three thousand population we found it a bit difficult to meet people. On enquiry, a villager made a remark that we should not have come during this period as majority of the households had migrated out for work. It was this initial revelation which made us curious about the existing reality of the village where large number of households seems to be looking for livelihood security elsewhere rather than their resources at home. The second incident which further reinforced our interest in the theme was again something to do with migration. This time it was not in the village but in a city. During a visit to Surat, the hub of migration, to understand the living and working conditions of the migrants, we met a migrant from Mahudi who made a very earnest plea with us. He said, 'why don't you do something and help us so that we do not have to migrate like this'. A visit to the appalling living places of the migrants in Surat was good enough to understand the reason behind the migrant's plea. It was a plea which was conveying both the physical and mental agony of a migrant. We needed no more convincing to understand the significance of the theme we had chosen for our study.

When we shared these reasons in a workshop, the late Prof. M.N. Srinivas, the doyen of Indian sociology, remarked that our selection of the theme is quite akin to what is normally done by the ethnographers. It is this combination of an ethnographer's curiosity as to why rural households from semi-arid areas are compelled to migrate in distress, and the concern of a development economist as to how such a migration could be reversed, what really made us work on this book. The book's focus is on finding why diversification has emerged as a coping strategy of the households in semi-arid villages; what is its real nature, what factors are causing it, and to what extent it can help address sustainability of livelihood. We hope the findings of the study would throw some light in understanding the real dynamics of the processes of diversification and help work towards ensuring better livelihood security for the poor.

The study, overall, has been a highly rewarding effort and exercise. The rewards were in terms of the opportunity we got to carry out a multi-disciplinary research and learn from the wisdom of villagers and host of other people with whom we could interact during the course of the study. All this has been made possible by the help and co-operation extended wholeheartedly by several people to us. It is our duty as well a pleasure to thank them all by recalling briefly various types of help rendered by them.

As mentioned above, the study was initiated with the support of NADEL of Swiss Federal Institute of Technology, Zurich from the funds received from Swiss National Science Foundation. We are highly thankful to Prof. Ruedi Baumgartner of NADEL who co-ordinated this multi-partner research project so ably and patiently which enabled the completion of the study. The separate grant of NADEL also has helped us in bringing out this book. We are thankful to all the concerned people at SDC, New Delhi and Bangalore who provided us the much needed support and logistics on the request of NADEL.

A major guiding force and motivator during the research study was the Rural Livelihood Systems (RLS) Forum, a semi-formal body consisting of the team members of all the partner institutions under the project. The regular and vibrant meetings of the Forum served as a platform for sharing all ideas and woes, personal as well as professional, which in a way helped in sustaining our real spirits.

We specially thank Prof. Ruedi Hogger (formerly with NADEL) who steered the RLS Forum, both academically and as a group, during the entire research period. We are highly indebted to all the members and family members of the Forum for their contributions and camaraderie. Our thanks to Profs. B.N. Hiremath, K.V. Raju and P. Thomas, and Mr. Anil Patel and Mr. Jasubhai Valand (all from IRMA); Prof. G. K. Karanth, Prof. G.S. Arora and Dr. Ramaswamy (from ISEC, Bangalore), and Mrs. Smita Premchander and Mr. Chidambaram (of SAMPARK, Bangalore). We express our sincere thanks to late Prof. M.N. Srinivas who very patiently listened to our presentation and made some highly relevant comments in one of the RLS

Forum workshops. We are highly indebted to all the participants of several RLS workshops for their valuable feedback and comments on the preliminary findings of the study. Our thanks also to the encouragement and critical comments of some of our colleagues on the work at IRMA – Profs. Vishwa Ballabh, Kameshwar Choudhary and Sukhpal Singh.

The real hard work of the study in terms of fieldwork, data gathering, data analysis and preparation of valuable field notes was put in by Mr. Anil P. Patel and Mr. Jasubhai Valand. We acknowledge with gratitude the untiring effort and help of these two gentlemen throughout the research project. We are also thankful to the research inputs received from Mr. Anand Srinivasan (a IRMA student) which helped in preparing the profile of Bodiya village.

We express our sincere thanks to Mr. Harnath Jagawat and his colleagues of Sadguru Water and Development Foundation (SWDF), Dahod; Mr. Sodhi and his colleagues of KRIBP (now GVT), Dahod; and the members of the Swadhyaya Parivar in Surendranagar district for their help extended in selecting the study villages and in conducting the fieldwork.

Our thanks to Prof. Katar Singh (ex-Director of IRMA) and Prof. K. Prathap Reddy, Director, IRMA for all the encouragement and support at various stages of the study. Incidentally, Prof. Katar Singh who was instrumental in getting the Project to IRMA also initiated the first author into the project through his constant encouragement.

We have received invaluable support from many other people at IRMA. Mrs. Rani Jayapalan painstakingly word processed multiple drafts of the book. She also helped in preparing the map and diagrams. Mrs. Vasantha Radhakrishnan and Mrs. Padmini Unnikrishnan also provided secretarial help in the initial stages. The accounts and estate departments arranged for all the logistics. We acknowledge sincerely their ungrudging help.

Our family members, though have borne the brunt of the long research project but still provided the much needed moral and other support constantly to sustain our spirits. We express our thanks to Manjula, Yashaswini and Jaynkar (of first author's family), and Satish and Raja (of second author's family).

The publication of the book in quick time has been made possible by the encouragement and support provided by Shri Ashok Kumar Mittal and his colleagues of Concept Publishing Company, New Delhi. Our sincere thanks to people at Concept Publishing Co.

Last but not the least, we mention here the wholehearted help received by us from the villagers of the three study villages—Mahudi, Mahunala and Bodiya. Though being strangers to them, the villagers had no hesitation in giving us data, care and affection whenever we made forays into their homes and villages. We even troubled them for data at their places of migration. It was always a response full of humility and equanimity from them. We are ever grateful to them for their co-operation.

Finally, we dedicate this book to the welfare of all the rural households who migrate in distress with the hope of leading a meaningful life one day.

H.S. Shylendra

Uma Rani

CONTENTS

LIST OF TABLES, MAP, DIAGRAMS AND BOXES

MAP

DIAGRAMS

BOXES

ABBREVIATIONS

RLS	Rural Livelihood Systems
NGO	Non-governmental Organisation
SWDF	Sadguru Water and Development Foundation
IRMA	Institute of Rural Management Anand
KRIBP	KRIBHCO Indo-British Rainfed Farming Project
PRA	Participatory Rural Appraisal
NSS	National Sample Survey
CPR	Common Property Resource
HYV	High Yielding Variety
JFM	Joint Forest Management

1

INTRODUCTION

1. INTRODUCTION

Even after five decades of planned development effort, the problem of rural poverty in India continues to pose a major policy challenge. Going by the official estimates for 1999-2000, 27.1 per cent of the rural population was living below poverty line in the country (Government of India 2002). In absolute figures this ratio accounts for about 193 million rural people.

In addressing this massive challenge of poverty, one of the strategies suggested is to focus policy attention on those areas or sections which are highly prone to poverty and deprivation. The semi-arid tropical areas are one such vulnerable areas which have been identified in the country needing such special attention for poverty alleviation and development (Walker and Ryan 1990). The semi-arid areas which are defined as those areas where the mean annual rainfall ranges from 400 mm to 1200 mm (*ibid.*) are considered to be both economically and ecologically highly fragile (Jodha 1995). They also account for a significant proportion of the rural poverty (Conroy *et al.* 2001).

The persistence of poverty in semi-arid areas has been attributed both to the failure of the various policy interventions to make any significant dent on poverty and also to the problem of degrading and depleting natural resources resulting in the inability of the local resource base to support a decent livelihood especially for the poor. One of the major policy failures has been the inappropriateness of the mainstream green revolution technology to suit the diverse and risk-prone conditions of semi-arid areas for a widespread adoption (Pretty 1995). As a result, agriculture in the large part of the semi-arid areas still remains largely under low-productivity and low output conditions aggravating the poverty situation. At the same time, even many of the programmes launched to tackle poverty directly focussing on the creation of self-employment and wage-employment have not yielded the desired results (Rath 1985; Neelakantan 1994).

Adding to the gravity of such failures in the semi-arid areas is the large scale degradation of natural resources caused by the depletion of forests, soil erosion, declining common pool resources, etc. (Jodha 1990). The impact of such degradation has been to further erode the livelihood support system making the poor who are dependent on them even more vulnerable. While policy interventions aimed at alleviating rural poverty continue with their mixed results; the poor on their own have been adopting various strategies to overcome their vulnerability. Such strategies of the poor have been very diverse across regions varying from tendency to overuse the already degraded common pool resources (*ibid.*, 1990) to diversification of the sources of livelihood by pursuing newer occupations including migrating seasonally to prosperous areas. There are evidence to suggest that diversification of occupation in fact seems to have become a major survival strategy of the poor in the semi-arid areas (Breman 1985; Subramanian and Hegde 1997; and Unni 1998). Seen from the above perspective, the process of occupational diversification taking place especially in the semi-arid areas, therefore, assumes added importance for addressing the problem of poverty as well as the closely linked issue of sustainability of the rural livelihood system.

2. UNDERSTANDING DIVERSIFICATION

Diversification may be broadly defined as a process wherein the rural households try to enlarge their sources of income and employment either due to the inability of the traditional sources to fully support their livelihood or due to newer opportunities arising out of the socio-economic changes occurring locally or externally.

The process of diversification is usually seen as a positive phenomenon, as it constitutes an important component of the economic growth process. The diversification and the resultant changing occupational structure in the developing countries have been viewed in the development literature from two perspectives (Koppel *et al.*, 1994; and Unni 1996). The first is the developmental perspective wherein the forces of economic growth like agricultural modernisation, urbanisation, and infrastructural development have led to the creation of new employment opportunities resulting in the emergence of a diversified occupational structure. The developmental forces operating through increased demand for inputs and goods and services have been able to attract or pull away the labour from the agricultural sector. The second perspective is the deterioration trajectory caused by factors inimical to development such as degradation of natural resources, agricultural stagnation and rapid population growth forcing livelihood diversification of a distress nature. The seasonal migration of the poor households to potential rural and urban areas in search of casual employment is considered to be a typical case of such distress diversification (Breman 1985). Alternatively, diversification also has been put forward as a residual sector hypothesis (Vaidyanathan 1986) which occurs when the rural labour is not fully employed by the agricultural sector and the non-agricultural sector may act as a sponge for absorbing the excess labour. Such a diversification may occur more in a situation where advanced stage of agricultural commercialization has been reached with widespread prevalence of wage labour system than in traditional rural communities having safeguards for livelihood security. Despite the diversification process being characterized based on the causal factors, delineating the factors which can help identify the real nature of diversification still remains a major challenge (Visaria and Basant 1994).

The rural employment scenario in India is characterised by a gradual shift towards non-farm occupations falling mainly in the tertiary sector (Visaria and Basant 1994). The bulk of the increase in the share of non-farm employment has taken place due to the increase in the proportion of casual non-agricultural workers. However, there are wide regional variations in the nature and pace of diversification. Much of the evidence about the changing employment scenario in India is provided by macro level studies which have attempted to explain the inter-regional and inter-temporal variations in the participation of the labour force in the non-farm activities. These macro level studies, however, fail to capture the real nature of occupational diversification taking place in different regions which are heterogeneous in nature. It is here an argument has been made for micro or region-specific studies which can throw light for clearly understanding the changing livelihood process (Vaidyanathan 1997).

The argument is further strengthened by the nature of evidence available from some of the micro level studies. These micro level studies suggest that diversification is taking place due to simultaneous operation of both the distress and developmental factors even in generally developed areas (Basant 1993; and Basant and Joshi 1994). Access to land, family size, caste, gender and educational status are some of the factors at the household level having a bearing on the nature and extent of diversification. Further, as identified by these studies, while there appears to be some positive impact of diversification as the enhanced household income has helped in overcoming the vulnerability; at the same time the degree of inequality in the income distribution across different sections seems to have widened in the process (Unni 1996).

Moreover, the rural labour processes including seasonal migration so far have been studied mainly from an agrarian angle (Koppel and Hawkins 1994). From such an angle, the changes in the occupational structure are considered to be an offshoot of the changes in the agrarian process. The demand for non-farm employment arises either due to the seasonality of agrarian operations or due to the declining agricultural surplus resulting from the declining yield or declining per capita land availability. It may also be due to the linkages created by commercialisation of agriculture by way of activities like supply of inputs and services, and marketing and processing of farm produce. Understanding diversification mainly from an agrarian angle is, however, considered narrow as it ignores the broader structural changes which influence the rural labour processes (Koppel and Hawkins 1994).

Rural occupational diversification is now being considered more as a derivative of a broader social, economic and political process. It is closely correlated both with the local processes involving changing social significance of the family, community and rural enterprises and with a wider processes involving the changing relationship between the State and the economic organisations of rural areas. Hence, it is emphasised that studies trying to explain the phenomenon of diversification must also try to incorporate perspectives which go beyond the narrow agrarian differentiation process. (Koppel and Hawkins 1994; and Vaidyanathan 1997).

The need for broad basing the studies on diversification from the above perspective is thus very well underscored. At the same time, a need has arisen for studies focusing on semi-arid areas to explore the relationship between diversification and the condition of natural resources given the emerging insight that regeneration of natural resources can have a positive impact in bringing down distress migration (Chopra and Gulati 1998). Very little attempt has been made to relate clearly the process of rural diversification to changes in the status of the natural resources such as land, water, forests, etc., which play a crucial role in determining the nature of livelihood strategies adopted by the rural households. The external interventions in natural resources, be it for the regeneration or exploitation, are also likely to bring into interplay the local reality with outside forces which are either supportive or inimical to the existing livelihood systems (Koppel and Hawkins 1994). It is here that the need arises to examine issues like: what role does the deterioration of natural resource base play in determining the demand for non-agricultural employment? and what is the likely impact of regeneration of natural resources like forests and water on the livelihood strategies of different sections of the rural community?

In the case of seasonal migration, which is one of the dominant modes of diversification adopted by the poor in the semi-arid tracts, there is a need to understand the phenomenon separately from the general process of diversification. Seasonal migration has certain peculiar dimensions both with regard to the causal factors and the nature of its impact on the livelihood. The large scale seasonal migration to urban areas has even come to be considered as a new kind of nomadism given the fact that labour from rural hinterlands has become an almost inexhaustible reservoir for the urban informal sector (Breman 1995).

The dominant theory on rural-urban migration views it as an individual utility maximisation behaviour arising out of the wage difference between the urban and rural sectors (Harris and Todaro 1970). Rural-urban migration is also considered as a risk spreading strategy of the family in the light of many local constraints faced on production (Stark and Lucas 1988). Whatever the explanation, it is argued that seasonal migration for the poor is more a matter of survival. It can in no way lead to any significant improvement in their livelihood particularly when it is distress driven. There are also attempts made to reverse the trend of distress migration which apparently goes against the general notion of migration being perceived as a positive phenomenon. Addressing the contradiction hence calls for understanding the phenomenon of seasonal migration different from the general diversification process. (See Chapter 2 for an elaboration of the arguments presented above).

3. HYPOTHESES FROM A MICRO STUDY

Given this context, we now look at the findings of an insightful micro study to develop the hypotheses for the present study. This was an exploratory study carried out in the first phase (1994-95) of the research project[1], 'Rural Livelihood Systems and Sustainable Natural Resource Management in Semi-arid Areas of India,' in a village called Mahudi in the Dahod district of Eastern Gujarat (Shylendra and Thomas 1996). The study revealed that the local livelihood has got diversified in a very significant way in the recent decades. A major form by which such a diversification has taken place is through seasonal migration of the labour force from the village to the prosperous urban and rural areas of Gujarat. About three-fourth of the households in Mahudi are found seeking employment outside the village to supplement their livelihood from the meagre agricultural base.

The study shows that to a large extent diversification has taken place due to distress factors like declining land availability, increasing population, and depletion of forests. At the same time, economic growth in other parts of Gujarat has opened up avenues for these households to seek alternative employment through migration. To many households in the village, seasonal migration seems to have

1. The research project was funded by the Swiss National Science Foundation, Zurich. Institute of Rural Management Anand (IRMA), Institute for Social and Economic Change (ISEC), Bangalore and NADELETH, Zurich were the main collaborating institutions in the Project.

become a major source of income and employment. The type of livelihood diversification similar to the one noticed in Mahudi has also been observed in many other parts of India (Subramanian and Hegde 1997). Such a large scale dependence on the external sources for employment would certainly have many ramifications on the local livelihood conditions. One could hence hypothesise here that:

The process of diversification as is unfolding in the semi-arid areas is likely to result in the emergence of rural livelihood systems which are dependent to a great extent on the external sources of livelihood for their sustenance with the local resources playing mainly a supplementary role. Depending on the extent and nature of the diversification, the process may have both positive and negative impacts and consequences on the livelihood conditions including the sustainable management of local resources. On the positive side, the diversification may ensure livelihood sustainability particularly for the poor. The assured means of livelihood support due to diversification might in turn lessen the pressure on the local resources. Because of the increased earnings from external sources, the tendency to intensively use the natural resources like land and forests may decline creating conditions for their sustainable use. Simultaneously, the new links established with the prosperous areas as a result may bring in additional resources and skills into the local economy resulting in the creation of new development opportunities. On the negative side, the local community because of its increased exposure to the outside culture may risk losing some of its own cherished identities. The migrating work force may be forced to bear with harsh working and living conditions resulting in overall poor quality of life. The growing external dependence might even reduce the households' interest to invest their human and capital resources to conserve or develop the local resources, be it owned privately or commonly. Unless the local alternatives are far more attractive than the earnings from the migration, there is only a reduced chance and incentive for the people to take any initiative for development of their resources.

The exploratory study also had some useful insights about the potential impact of developmental interventions on distress diversification. In the village, there have been many interventions made both by the government and the non-government agencies aimed at improving the livelihood through regeneration of natural resource base, asset creation, employment generation, etc. The non-government organizations (NGOs) functioning in the area had an explicit objective of arresting the phenomenon of distress migration of the local population through their interventions in natural resource regeneration. The initial assessment of the intervention in water harvesting made in the village by Sadguru Water and Development Foundation (SWDF), an NGO functioning in the area, revealed that the intervention seems to have made an impact by way of intensification of agriculture and reduced seasonal migration. Based on similar impacts in other villages, the NGO also claimed that through their programmes like water resource development and agro-forestry they have been quite successful in bringing down distress migration in the region. However, the study revealed that though this may be true in pockets of NGO intervention; bulk of the households which are outside the purview of the NGO programme continue to depend on seasonal migration for livelihood security in the absence of any other viable alternatives.

In the context of such an impact observed, it may be hypothesized that:

A desirable strategy for the developmental agencies in such areas is to take cognizance of the reality of migration and work not only towards creating conditions which can help arrest the trend but also try to improve the condition of the migrants as long as distress migration continues. This may include taking initiatives such as regeneration of local natural resources for improving the livelihood as well as helping the migrants to bargain for better working and living conditions at the place of migration. At the same time, the agencies may also try and tap the positive dimensions of growing rural-urban linkages like inflow of income and development of new skills, for betterment of the local livelihood. Such an approach, in the long run may help in attaining a more sustainable livelihood for the poor in the semi-arid tracts in the context of growing diversification.

4. OBJECTIVES AND METHODOLOGY OF THE STUDY

Given this hypotheses raised above based on the insights from the exploratory study and the major research issues identified with regard to diversification, the main goal of the present study is:

To better understand the links between the growing occupational diversification, changing conditions of local natural resources and issues concerning sustainability of rural livelihood systems in semi-arid areas. From such an improved understanding, policy implications are to be drawn for developmental agencies as to their future stance towards interventions for livelihood improvement including bringing down distress seasonal migration.

More specifically, the study has the following objectives:

i. To study the nature and magnitude of the process of occupational diversification and the growing external dependence of rural livelihood systems in the semi-arid areas particularly in the context of a changing natural resource base;
ii. To examine the factors influencing the rural households to diversify and to assess the role and impact of the interventions particularly those aimed at improving the livelihood. How successful are these interventions in reversing the process of distress diversification?; and
iii. To analyse the implications of the diversification and growing rural-urban linkages for issues concerning the sustainability of rural livelihoods. What are the households' changing perceptions and practices about

the management of natural resources owned privately or commonly? What are the possibilities of harnessing the positive aspects of diversification for improving the local livelihood systems?

The major focus of the present study is to gain a micro-level understanding of the various dimensions of the phenomenon of diversification among the households in the semi-arid areas. The present study though carried out independently by the authors, forms a part of the larger collaborative research study mentioned above and carried out at Institute of Rural Management, Anand (IRMA) in two phases during 1994-2000. Besides the present theme on diversification, two more themes namely, the role of agricultural technology for livelihood security and understanding motivations for collective action also have been pursued under the overall research study. The criteria for selection of research sites have been determined mainly based on the goals of the larger study aimed at understanding the changing livelihood strategies of households and the impact of development interventions in semi-arid areas. The villages selected for the larger study have served as common research sites for all the three themes. Keeping the three themes in mind, it was decided that in addition to Mahudi, selected for the exploratory study in the first phase, two more semi-arid villages, Mahunala and Bodiya, in Gujarat were selected for the purpose. While Mahudi and Mahunala are villages inhabited by the tribal Bhil population, Bodiya is a non-tribal multi-caste village. The diverse types of villages were selected mainly to compare and contrast the livelihood strategies of communities in different socio-economic settings.

The above three villages were selected for the larger study mainly because of the nature of interventions made in these villages. The village Mahudi in Jhalod taluka of Dahod district was selected with the help of SWDF, an NGO based in Dahod, which has made various interventions for regeneration of natural resources like water and forests in the village. The village Mahunala which shares with Mahudi all the major demographic and agro-climatic characteristics was selected with the help of another Dahod based development agency called KRIBHCO Indo-British Rainfed Farming Project (KRIBP)[2] which was implementing, among other things, a participatory agricultural extension programme in the region. The village Mahunala, located in the Limkheda taluka of Dahod district, was selected to gain a wider understanding of the livelihood in the region along with Mahudi. The village Bodiya, located in the Surendranagar district falling under the Saurashtra region of Gujarat, was selected mainly because of the presence of a socio-religious reform movement called *Swadhyaya*. Under the movement, simple innovative and participatory ways of conserving and regenerating natural resources are being tried out mainly by appealing to certain moral values of the individuals.

As per the agro-climatic regions identified for Gujarat by the Planning Commission (1991), all the three villages are located in semi-arid regions (see Map 1.1). The villages Mahudi and Mahunala come under the middle Gujarat region having an annual average rainfall of 904 mm. The village Bodiya falls in north Saurashtra region with an annual average rainfall of 537 mm (*ibid.*).

A mix of research tools has been used for the study consisting of questionnaire based sample survey of households, Participatory Rural Appraisal (PRA) tools, indepth case studies and informal focus group discussions. Adequate care has been taken to ensure that the households selected as far as possible represent different segments and interest groups in the study villages. Further, all the major issues of the study have been examined by interacting wherever possible both with the male and female members of the households in order to obtain a balanced view.

2. The Project since then been transformed into an organization called Gram Vikas Trust based in Dahod.

Map 1.1: Location of Study Villages

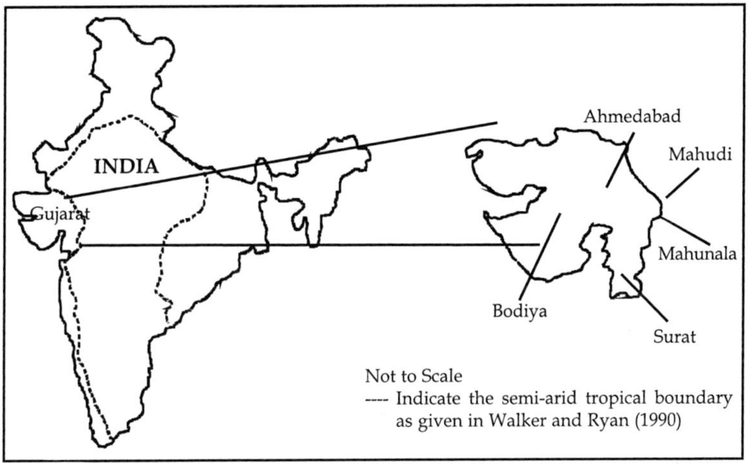

In Mahudi, an attempt has been made to build further on the database of the exploratory study. Besides making use of the data from the exploratory study based on a baseline survey of 316 households, the changing livelihood scenario in Mahudi has been captured by a repeat survey of 45 households covered under the baseline survey. Out of these 45 households, 22 were from the area where SWDF has made its intervention for harnessing the village river by way of building a checkdam; the other 23 households were selected from the other areas of the village not covered under the above intervention. The main purpose of selecting such a sample in Mahudi consisting of households coming under both the intervention and non-intervention areas was to make an assessment of the impact of the intervention on the livelihood conditions. The survey data has been supplemented with informal group discussions and indepth case studies of few households carried out subsequent to the survey in the second phase.

In Mahunala, the intervening agency, KRIBP had developed a fairly good baseline data about various socio-economic aspects of the village collected through PRA and other tools. To avoid duplication of the data collection, it was decided to make use of some of the relevant data and information about Mahunala gathered by KRIBP. However, to gain a first hand insight into the livelihood conditions in Mahunala, a survey of 20 households accounting for about ten per cent of the total households in the village was conducted and it was followed by informal group discussions and household case studies.

In the multi-caste Bodiya village, a survey of 66 sample households was carried out. The sample accounted for about one-third of the total households in the village covering different caste groups broadly in proportion to their strength in the total households. The survey data was supplemented by informal group discussions with different communities in the village and indepth case study of a few households.

As the focus of the present study is also on capturing the dimension of rural-urban linkages influencing the nature of diversification, a study of the living and working conditions of the migrants in places of their migration like Ahmedabad, Nadiad, Anand, and Surat was also carried out. Informal interactions and discussions were held with the migrants for the purpose.

The informal group discussions, household case studies, and interactions with the migrants were carried out at different times during the period 1997-99.

Though the purpose of carrying out household surveys in all three villages was to collect quantitative data needed for examining the research questions raised, attempt has been made wherever possible to supplement the quantitative data with qualitative insights about various aspects of livelihood gathered from formal and informal interactions with the households. The use of such multiple research methods including some unconventional ones is the major strength of the present study in analysing the phenomenon of diversification.

5. THE CONCEPT OF SUSTAINABLE LIVELIHOOD

The methodology and the approach followed for understanding the phenomenon of diversification has been made possible mainly by the adoption of a heuristic kind of a conceptual framework for understanding the rural livelihood system. The framework adopted under the larger study also has been adopted here as it gives scope for exploring livelihood in a holistic manner.

The livelihood framework adopted under the larger research study (Hogger 2000) tries to depict the livelihood system, be that of an individual or a family or a community, in the form of a Nine-Square Mandala (See Diagram 1.1) encompassing a nine-fold focus ranging from the purely materialistic outer realities like physical resources, skills, socio-economic space and institutions to the non-materialistic inner realities of life like emotions, orientations and attitudes. According to the framework, livelihood is defined as 'everything that provides continuity and meaning to the life of a family or a community'[3] (Hogger 2000). Thus, livelihood is viewed as a holistic concept which encompasses forces operating both on psychic and physical planes having a bearing on the survival, identity, and continuity of the system. The approach basically insists on exploring all important factors, be they fall in the material or non-material plain of life, for understanding livelihood. For example, studying migration pattern may require analyzing not only the local food and employment situation of the migrants but also the cultural and emotional factors attached with the movement of labour.

3. Incidentally, the meaning of livelihood given under the framework finds similarity with the meaning of the term used for the livelihood by the local community in one of the study villages (Mahudi). The local community use the term *'Ghar Chalava'* meaning 'keep the household going' whenever it comes to discussing any issue related to livelihood.

Diagram 1.1: A Multi-Dimensional Livelihood Framework

9. Individual Orientation	8. Family Orientation	7. Collective Orientation
6. Inner Human Space	5. Family Space	4. Socio-economic space
3. Emotional Base	2. Knowledge and Activity Base	1. Physical Base

Inner reality ⟷ Outer reality

The holistic approach to rural livelihood adopted here finds similarity with other recent approaches (Scoones 1998, Chambers 1987) which also emphasise on broadening the meaning of livelihood. According to the new approaches, livelihood has to be looked at not only from the point of view of household capabilities, assets—material and social, and activities which are required as a means of living but also in terms of opportunities and strategies available for livelihood improvement. (Scoones 1998). Taking such a broad approach to livelihood has been largely necessitated as the earlier approaches focused too narrowly on any one issue like income or employment ignoring the scope for multi-dimensional strategy for ensuring livelihood security. Moreover, the earlier approaches to livelihood tended to ignore the concerns of vulnerable sections like women. The new approach has brought into the perspective the need to address the concept of livelihood also from the point of view of such concerns (Chambers 1997; Sarin 1997).

Having taken a broader view of the concept of livelihood, a similar holistic approach has been adopted in the study for understanding the concept of livelihood sustainability. Based on the definitions given by Jodha (1995) and Scoones (1998), the sustainability of a livelihood system (household or community) has been defined here as the ability of the system to cope up with stresses and shocks and at the same time to maintain and enhance its productivity or performance on a long term basis. In doing so, the system may either draw upon its own resources or establish necessary linkages with the outside systems without affecting in the process the potentiality of the local resources and other means to contribute towards attaining livelihood security and improvement. The major advantage of this definition lies in its ability to offer a consistent framework for integrating various elements of sustainability (Jodha 1995). There is enough scope for the livelihood system to be dynamic and be compatible with development. It can also address the issue of both inter-generational and intra-generational equity through its emphasis on maintaining the ability of the resource base to take care of both the current and future needs. The inter-system linkages envisaged also breaks any constraints imposed on an isolated livelihood system.

6. CHAPTER SCHEME

The book is organized into seven chapters including the present one detailing the scope and objectives of the study. Chapter 2 provides a critical review of the available theoretical and empirical literature on occupational diversification and rural-urban migration and tries to identify major research issues for the study. Chapter 3 deals with the nature and impact of occupational diversification in two tribal villages of Mahudi and Mahunala. The nature and impact of occupational diversification in the multi-caste Bodiya village is analysed in Chapter 4. Chapter 5 makes an attempt to look at the rural-urban linkage aspect of diversification with a focus on two dominant non-farm activities, viz. construction work and diamond polishing observed in the study villages. Chapter 6 tries to make an assessment of the potential impact of a developmental intervention made by an NGO on reversing the distress migration in the village Mahudi. Chapter 7 presents the summary and conclusions of the study.

2

OCCUPATIONAL DIVERSIFICATION AND RURAL-URBAN MIGRATION IN INDIA: SOME EVIDENCE[1]

1. INTRODUCTION

Occupational diversification in an economy is usually considered to be a positive development as it is an important component of the growth process. The various population censuses and National Sample Survey (NSS) rounds in India suggest a growing trend, albeit slowly, of diversification in rural areas in recent decades by way of an increase in the share of rural non-agricultural sector in the total workforce (Basant and Kumar 1989 and Sundaram 2001). A clear understanding of the phenomenon of occupational diversification can help address the following issues:

i. What drives demand for non-agricultural employment by different types of rural households? How are different forms of employment influenced by levels and forms of agricultural development? What are the terms of employment for non-agricultural rural work and how do these terms relate to social and political relationships within and outside the rural areas? Under what conditions is diversification in rural areas a

1. An earlier version of this Chapter appeared as an article in *Journal of Social and Economic Development*, Vol. IV, No. 1, Jan.-June 2002, 27-41.

fundamentally positive factor in the survival of the poorest groups? (Koppel and Hawkins 1994).

ii. What has been the role of various natural resources like land, forests, and water in supporting and determining the livelihood of different sections of rural community? In what way the changes in the natural resource base bring about changes in the occupational structure? In what way and to what extent interventions for regeneration of natural resources are likely to have an impact which can strengthen the occupational base?

iii. When diversification has a strong urban linkage, studies focusing on the linkage would help address the impact of urbanisation on rural poverty, investment, savings behaviour and labour market development in rural areas. Further, one would also be able to get an insight into the nature of urban informal labour markets which are dominated by migrant rural workers (Breman 1996). The question of bringing about balanced rural-urban growth also depends upon understanding such a linkage.

iv. What are the directions of impact of policies aimed at bringing about rural diversification and development? What are the best strategies, short term as well as long term, which can bring about balanced and equitable growth particularly in the context of distress rural diversification?

The present chapter is an attempt to critically review some of the available theoretical and empirical studies in the area of occupational diversification and rural-urban migration both in order to get an answer to some of the above questions and to identify, based on the gaps, issues for further research.

2. THEORETICAL PERSPECTIVES

The process of changing rural occupational structure in the

developing countries is viewed in the development literature from two perspectives (Koppel *et al.*, 1994, Unni 1996). The first is the development perspective wherein the forces of economic growth, such as agricultural modernisation, urbanisation, etc., have led to creation of newer job opportunities leading to the emergence of a diversified occupational structure. This growth process, first analysed by Kuznets (1966), is mediated by agricultural transformation, attendant upon the mechanisation of agriculture accompanied by a rise in the productivity of agricultural labour and its surplussing. The notion behind the argument is that the growth of agricultural production and productivity may create a surplus which may be invested in non-agricultural enterprises, where an increase in rural incomes due to agricultural prosperity may alter the pattern of demand for goods and services. Both the generation of agricultural surplus and a changing pattern of consumption demand could lead to an increase in demand for labour in the non-agricultural sector (Unni 1994). At a subsequent stage of development, the increase in the demand for services from both the primary and the secondary sectors leads to the growth of tertiary sector. The expansion of the non-farm sector is, in Kuznets' scheme, prosperity-induced. Alternatively, it is also highly plausible that this agricultural prosperity will lead to an increase in demand for labour in agriculture, leading to a better absorption of labour therein and there would be less spill-over of excess labour into non-agricultural employment (Vaidyanathan 1986).

In sharp contrast to the first perspective, McGee's (1971) thesis is sceptical of the growth prospects afforded by agricultural labour and industrial transformation. For McGee, the surplussing of the agricultural labour is more pertinently seen as a consequence of agrarian distress—a surplus that finds no ready absorption into productive employment in an industrial sector whose absorptive capacity is limited. The surplus labour is then confronted with no option but to settle into a low-productivity tertiary sector. This expansion of the non-farm sector, from McGee's perspective, is distress-induced. Seasonal migration of the poorer households to urban areas in search of unskilled employment in informal sector can be considered a typical case of such distress diversification. The deterioration trajectory is caused by factors inimical to growth and prosperity such as degradation and depletion of the natural resource base, agricultural stagnation and rapid population growth compelling livelihood diversification of a distress nature.

This distress diversification has been alternatively put forward as residual sector hypothesis (Vaidyanathan 1986) which occurs when labour is not fully absorbed in the agricultural sector and the non-agricultural sector acts as a sponge for the excess labour. In this context, Sheila Bhalla (1989) identifies two kinds of distress diversification in which non-agricultural rural activities become residual labour force absorbers. The first is the case of supplementary workers who have no main occupation, but engage in some subsidiary work to supplement household income. The second is the case of persons with a main occupation who also engage in secondary activity.

Thus, two types of phenomena contribute to the growth of the non-agricultural sector: those representing development, captured by variables such as agricultural productivity, growth of income, infrastructure development, urbanisation and commercialisation; and others relating to distress reflected in variables such as unemployment and poverty.

3. SOME EMPIRICAL STUDIES

The empirical studies supporting the development trajectory have been that of Unni (1994) and Dev (1994) who show that there exists a positive relation between agricultural development and the proportion of rural non-agricultural workers. Their analysis is based on the NSS data, and the relationship appears stronger when the share of rural non-agricultural workers is regressed on the per hectare agricultural productivity. This evidence supports the hypothesis of Vaidyanathan (1986), who shows a significant positive relationship of the share of rural non-agricultural workers with rural prosperity, by taking agricultural output per capita of agricultural population as an indicator. Further, analysing the rural non-agricultural employment in India based on the NSS and Censuses data, Basant and Kumar (1989) suggest that during the last three decades, the share of the rural non-agricultural sector in the total rural work force has increased. They show that it is primarily the casual workers who shift from agricultural activities to non-agricultural activities during slack agricultural seasons. Emphasising on the seasonality aspect, their study provides evidence to suggest that the involvement of labour in non-agricultural activities occurs countercyclically to the demands of the agricultural calendar and it results in labour flows between the rural agricultural and non-agricultural sector.

Jayaraj (1992), using the Census data for 1171 villages across 11 talukas of Tamilnadu, tries to determine the possible factors or determinants which affect the level of non-agricultural employment. The author adopts a broad framework which includes both the development and distress perspectives. The basic focus is on the spatial variations in the incidence of non-farm employment which are both internal and external to the rural economy. The study shows that the phenomenon of non-agricultural employment is not only as much a function of agrarian prosperity as of agrarian distress but it also a case that prosperity, like distress, could either promote or inhibit the growth of agricultural sector.

Much of the evidence about the growth of non-agricultural employment in India pertains to macro level, based on NSS and Censuses data which fail to capture the real nature of non-agricultural employment prevailing in different regions as they are highly heterogeneous in nature. This apart the activities also differ depending upon the levels of agricultural growth in different regions, and these complexities cannot be captured or observed at macro or meso level. Another issue that has been identified in regard to analysis based on the secondary data is the apprehension about its reliability and adequacy. Bhalla (1996) cautions about the use of NSS data as perhaps the sample size of the NSSO surveys are inadequate to capture the secular changes in the structure of the workforce. In regard to reliability, Bhalla points out the fact that the employment questions were introduced into the demographic block of a questionnaire on consumption expenditure. Thus, in order to understand the dynamism that exists in the rural areas with regard to the nature of diversification, one has to look more towards micro-level studies.

Basant (1993), in a micro level study of 30 villages in five districts of Gujarat, looks at diversification among the different households across the different income groups. For households which did not operate any land, the income from the non-farm activities (72 per cent) seemed to be the major source than those who operated with land (40 per cent). Diversification by the households involved their participation in different activities and also involvement in multiple economic activities by a single worker. Diversification into different activities by the households was influenced by their access to land, family size, and nearness of the village to a town.

Basant and Joshi (1994) provide micro-level evidence of diversification of the development kind, where the agriculturists invest their surplus in non-agricultural activities, especially in activities like processing and trade, in the agriculturally developed six villages of Kheda district in Gujarat. The study basically establishes the linkage that exists between agricultural prosperity, commercialisation and urbanisation, on one hand and, the growth of rural non-agricultural employment on the other.

The study further shows that the growth of rural non-agricultural sector is linked to agricultural prosperity and commercialisation mainly in large villages because of the relatively large internal market. The analysis also shows how distress and development factors can operate simultaneously in the same region. At the same time, the study reveals that the identification of distress diversification is complicated at the micro-level because, shifts to non-agricultural activities out of distress may take various forms. The data show that both the households with large land holdings and the landless contribute to the non-agricultural work force in the region. This means that diversification takes place at both ends of the spectrum; with landed households diversifying into productive non-agricultural activities like trade and agro-processing, and the poor into the less productive non-agricultural activities, like casual wage labour.

Jayaraj (1996) observes that households with access to land enjoy relatively better access to non-agricultural employment in his micro-level study in the North Arcot district of Tamilnadu. He tries to develop a coherent framework where the development of the rural non-agricultural sector is viewed as one of the components of the overall socio-economic transformation, and analyses spatial and temporal variations in the incidence of rural non-agricultural employment. Given this framework, he finds that gender, caste, and land limit the access to employment in non-agricultural sector, while education helps to get better access to employment in the non-agricultural sector.

Occupational diversification of the development kind is observed in yet another micro-level study. Kumar (1996) argues that with economic growth, there has been a relative shift away from agriculture towards industry and services in Bhuvel, a village in the developed pocket of Kheda district in Gujarat. Occupational diversification has taken place even among the landless households, such as artisan and scheduled castes who have diversified into various economic activities such as government services and other odd jobs in factories and shops. Sharan and Dayal (1996) also observe this kind of occupational diversification of the marginalised sections of the society among the Ghasis of Ranchi.

In the context of non-agricultural employment being an alternative for sustainable rural livelihoods, a micro-level study by Unni (1996) in two talukas, irrigated and semi-arid in Mehsana district of Gujarat indicates that non-agricultural activities have a positive impact on rural livelihoods in various ways. Besides, enhancing the household's income in general, it enables the agricultural households to survive year-to-year weather fluctuations. She observes that the non-agricultural employment strengthens the base of rural livelihoods, through increase in incomes, but also increase the degree of inequality in the distribution of rural income.

The studies reviewed above reveal that as agricultural growth takes place and its base expands, it results in the linkage effect through increased demand for farm inputs, farm services and consumer goods which are strong enough to raise non-farm employment. This results in a positive relation between the level of agricultural development and non-farm employment. Further, these studies have observed that the diversification of the development kind also could be due to higher levels of education and increasing accumulation of capital. However, the studies reviewed above have mainly focused on the developed pockets. Hence, the strong evidence in support of the development phenomenon. One needs to also look at how in backward areas the expansion of non-agricultural employment reflects a situation in which agriculture is unable to provide sufficient livelihood support for the rural population and forces many of them, the rural poor in particular, to diversify their employment channels for sheer survival (Shylendra and Thomas, 1995).

4. NEED FOR A NEW FOCUS

Macro-level studies are concerned mainly with the

description and explanation of inter-regional and inter-temporal variations in the participation of households in non-farm activities. Further, the available evidence on occupational diversification shows a complex pattern of different activities undertaken in rural areas, with varying degrees of emphasis on farm and non-farm work. What is also important for understanding the determinants of economic diversification in rural areas is the impact of the structure and functioning of the labour markets. The economy functions in an integrated way wherein agriculture and non-agriculture sector are inter-linked and rural and urban areas are closely interdependent (Bharadwaj 1989; Unni 1994). Most of the empirical studies at the macro and micro-levels mainly indicate that occupational diversification is a result of the changes in the agrarian processes. From this angle, diversification arises either due to seasonality of agrarian operations or due to declining agricultural surplus resulting from declining yield or declining per capita land availability, or due to linkage effects created by commercialisation of agriculture by way of demand for activities like supply of inputs and services, marketing and processing of agricultural produce. In the current debate this view is considered narrow from the point of view of capturing the total reality of the rural labour processes as it ignores the broader structural changes which are influencing rural labour differentiation (Koppel and Hawkins 1994).

Hence, studies trying to explain the phenomenon of diversification must incorporate perspectives which go beyond the narrow agrarian differentiation process (Koppel and Hawkins 1994; Vaidyanathan 1997). It is important not only to develop a comprehensive analytical framework that captures factors operating on both demand and supply side of non-agricultural employment but also look at outcomes in terms of level of non-agricultural employment, wage rates, incomes (Vaidyanathan 1997) and more so on impact of diversification on poverty (Unni 1998). In this context the perspective to be considered could be a derivative of a broader social, economic and political process closely correlated both with local processes involving changing social significance of the family, community and rural enterprises with wider processes involving the changing relationship between the State and the economic organisation of rural areas (Koppel and Hawkins 1994).

5. NATURAL RESOURCES AND OCCUPATIONAL DIVERSIFICATION

In the literature on diversification not much of an attempt has been made to relate clearly the process of occupational diversification to changes in the status of the natural resource base. Natural resources such as land, water and forest which could be either common or private property resources, play a crucial role in determining the nature of livelihood strategies adopted by the rural households and the resultant occupational structure. At the same time, outside interests and interventions in natural resources are likely to bring into play the local livelihood system with external factors which are either inimical to or supportive of the existing livelihood system (Koppel and Hawkins 1994).

The existing studies in the area of occupational diversification and natural resource management have mainly tried to focus on what role the changing resource base can play in bringing about occupational diversification, the impact of such diversification on the management or development of local natural resources and how interventions in natural resources regeneration can change the process of diversification, particularly of a distress nature. Occupational diversification or distress migration from rural areas can sometimes result from environmental degradation. Breman (1985) observes that in the semi-arid areas of South Gujarat, forestry work was a major source of employment for the tribals during the slack agricultural seasons. However, since the significance of this source of income and employment has declined sharply as a result of deforestation during the last few decades, outmigration from these villages to urban areas for alternative source of employment during the slack agricultural seasons has increased over the years.

Chopra and Gulati (1997) address the question of regenerating the natural resources by defining common property rights in the arid and semi-arid region of Western India where prevailing outmigration stems largely from push factors such as environmental degradation and decrease in common land. They establish, through a simultaneous equation system, that a higher extent of outmigration depicts a higher level of environmental degradation. Regeneration of natural resource base, therefore, would help in reducing migration. The authors emphasise that in the case of common resources like land, if property rights are well defined with the help of proper institutional arrangements and outside intervention, labour would move towards creation of common assets. This would bring about an improvement in the environment leading to a decrease in outmigration. Hence, the same resources support higher levels of population.

Further, Chopra and Gulati (1998) in their micro-level study show how institutional creation in common property resources influences distance migration. Basing their analysis on the work done by two NGOs in Rajasthan, the authors observe that the creation of common property rights significantly slows down distance migration. Out migration and participation in Common Property Resource (CPR) management are interrelated. Institutional build-up improves participation in management of commons, helping to reduce distress migration.

Similarly, the study by Balooni and Singh (1994) in the Panchmahals districts of Gujarat also shows how intervention by outside agency can help in reversing seasonal migration. The study shows that intervention by an NGO in a lift irrigation scheme in 1976 and later in a farm forestry programme in 1982 helped the tribals of a semi-arid backward village to transform from a resource poor to a highly productive area. This intervention not only provided the tribals additional income from trees and crop output but also increased their number of days of local employment. This additional income and employment generation resulted in lowering the rate of seasonal migration from 75 per cent in 1976 to 5 per cent in 1993.

Given the above finding, it therefore becomes important to understand clearly the role played by natural resources in supporting rural livelihoods and in determining the demand for non-agricultural employment. Another critical question which needs to be addressed, particularly from the point of view of policy is, what is the likely impact of regeneration of natural resources like forests and land on the livelihood strategies of different sections of the rural community?

6. RURAL-URBAN MIGRATION

The last few decades have observed massive seasonal or permanent migration of peasants from rural to urban areas in the third world countries. The migration from rural to urban areas has been extensively documented and there has also been an enormous growth of theoretical literature and empirical evidence towards understanding the realities of rural-urban migration (de Haan 2000). The phenomenon has also led to a considerable debate on the process of capitalist penetration into rural areas and the role played by it in influencing the existing socio-economic differentiation in the countryside.

One of the prominent theoretical arguments on rural-urban migration views it as an individual utility maximisation behaviour (Todaro 1969; Hariss and Todaro 1970), where wage differentials between the urban and rural sector is considered to be the prime determinant of migration. The neo-classical expected income model of Todaro, with its numerous variants, seems to focus on individual potential migrants, and argues that holding much less constant, people will migrate if they expect to do better than they probably would if they did not move. The neo-classical theory of migration is largely based on the Lewis model, where the institutionally given urban wage rate and the wage differential between the urban and the rural sector forms the basis of framework. This implies that migration from the rural to the urban sector results when actual rural wage rate falls short of the expected urban wage rate. The neo-classical model which has become the most dominant framework in the context of rural-urban migration, however, assumes that the rural migrants are a homogeneous category of poor people, ignoring the fact that their migration is not always based on a strategy of maximisation, but of survival. The circulation of labour or migration from rural to urban areas is not always a voluntary process but at times it is a response to economic necessity. The Todaro model does not consider the non-economic factors such as pressure of population, inequalities in the distribution of land owning and other institutional mechanisms which lead to migration from rural to urban areas. An application of Todaro's model of rural-urban migration for all-India and three major States, Maharashtra, Tamilnadu and West Bengal, did not provide enough evidence to support the hypothesis that rural-urban migration takes place primarily in response to expected income differentials (Sundaram 1986).

Breman (1985) also criticises the Todaro model by taking the case of a large-scale displacement of labour in the tribal hinterland of South Gujarat. His study shows how the migrants who find work in the cotton ginning factories in Bardoli (migrant place) earn a lower daily wage than the labourers remaining behind in Valod (originating place) to work on roads or canals there. Breman's study concludes that seasonal migration is a matter of survival or, at best, of consolidation, and hardly ever results in accumulation or reinvestment in the home area.

Alternatively, inter-temporal family contract models of migration also have been constructed (Stark 1980; Stark and Bloom 1985; Stark and Lucas 1988). These models emphasise on risk spreading (Stark and Levari 1982) by families in the presence of imperfections in rural capital markets (Stark 1982) as a strategy to overcome constraints on production and investment activities as a result of missing or incomplete credit and insurance markets in rural areas. The basic premise of these alternative models which are based on household utility maximisation is that the decision to migrate is not taken by an individual but the family members also have a role to play. Stark and Lucas (1988) suggest that labour migration by one or more family members can be an effective mechanism to self-finance local production activities and acts as a self-insurance against local income risks. Stark and Levari (1982) and Taylor (1986) also argue that migration plays a risk-reducing and insurance-enhancing role in production and investment decisions. Hoddinott (1994) models migration as an outcome of a joint utility maximisation by the prospective migrant and the other family members. These models of behavioural decision-making thus emphasise that circulation of labour is a form of risk reduction by spreading the risk spatially and occupationally while maximising family consumption.

Apart from testing the validity of the above developed models, the discussion on rural-urban migration in India seems to have focussed on determining the relative importance of push and pull factors in inducing migration. Income differentials are seen as the major pull factors; while seasonality risk, market failures, erosion of assets and landlessness are seen as push factors. Most of these studies have also tried to address the demographic aspects of migration (Gupta 1984, Kundu 1986, and Oberai and Singh 1980). Their analysis is based on NSS and Censuses data on regional as well as all-India levels, depicting the extent and magnitude of migration from rural to urban areas. However, a major limitation of studies based on secondary data is that they do not throw any light on the changes in economic conditions, including consumption and lifestyle, that migrants undergo in urban areas to adapt themselves to their new environment. Besides, such studies also fail to capture the problems the migrants face in leaving the security provided by the family, the community, well-established patterns of work, economic and social relationships, to live and work in a harsh and hostile environment and among people most of whom are strangers.

Dasgupta and Laishley (1975) have tried to identify the social, economic and demographic factors in village life associated with migratory movements and who really are the migrants. Their work reveals that factors related to both village base and urban relations induce migration. The factors they identify at the village base are land shortage, low fertility of land, skewed distribution of land and the resulting high proportion of landless agricultural workers. The two major urban-related factors that they identify are commercialisation of agriculture and access to towns.

A major study in the area of migration has been that of Connell *et al.* (1976), which tries to understand migration as an imbalance in the access to resources that exists between regions, families and villages. It examines the conditions that influence the decision to migrate, the destination, occupations pursued income from migration and the other social and economic characteristics of the migrants. The study shows that it is the inadequate access to income generating land in the village and the hope to improve the living conditions in the village that encourages households or individuals to migrate. The migration that they document is seasonal, circular and permanent in nature.

The study also documents in detail the benefits of remittances, the expenditure pattern of the migrants and their preferences over the usage of the remittances. The expenditure pattern of the remittances, as per the study, reflects the poverty and the resultant lack of investment opportunities that the migrants are faced with. They observe that the remittances are utilised mainly for meeting everyday household needs, and when basic requirements are met, remittances often flow into conspicuous consumption. It was observed among several agricultural labour migrants from Eastern Uttar Pradesh to Punjab in 1973 that the income from remittances is mainly used to defray consumer debt in their home villages so as to avoid the need to sell land. In many villages the level of investment into agriculture was found to be very low. The pattern of investment shows that some of the households invested their remittances in education, thus stimulating further migration. Another major usage of remittances is for payment of bride price which exists in some villages. The study also revealed that remittances are not just an economic phenomenon but involve a social angle wherein they become an instrument for migrant households to seek a continued stake in the village economy and social hierarchy.

As regards the impact due to absence of migrants, the study observes that the negative impact of male emigration on agricultural production is reduced if women normally do farmwork or can move into it easily; but a large emigration can produce a drastic shortage of men. This would lead to a shift to easy crops of low value, at least until migrants return with more favourable adaptations or remittances.

Breman (1985), based on his study of seasonal migrants in South Gujarat observes that for the tribal population, seasonal migration is more of a 'holding operation', which enables them by and large to maintain their relative positions in the village and to avoid alienation of land as far as possible. The continued migration for the past few decades has brought about little or no improvement in the quality of tribal life, particularly for the large and the growing under-privileged. Yet the cash income derived from labour outside the home area is not in itself enough for keeping one step ahead of the danger of social and economic deterioration. In this context, one could probably try and probe the question that the study by Connell *et al.* (1976) poses, viz., that labour migration stems from a situation of inequality, but are the existing socio-economic differences also increasing as a result of this?

Seasonal migration of the kind referred to by Breman represents diversification, particularly of the distress nature. Unlike in the case where the households diversify induced by the process of economic growth, diversification by way of seasonal migration has certain peculiar dimensions both in terms of the causal factors and its impact. This makes it necessary to understand the phenomenon separately from the general process of diversification. Apart from the foregoing questions about seasonal migration, there is also the issue of harsh reality of migrants working and living in inhuman conditions (Breman 1996), raising questions about the desirability of the whole process. Such concerns have further led to arguments for arresting or reversing the phenomenon. In fact, developmental agencies working in areas where such seasonal migration is widely prevalent normally aim at reducing migration by appropriate interventions. Though such a policy stance goes against the general notion of migration as a positive phenomenon, it is precisely such policy arguments which call for a better understanding of seasonal migration (Shylendra and Uma Rani 2000). In what context does migration needs to be reversed and in what context a proactive stance may be taken?

7. CONCLUSION

The phenomenon of occupational diversification, given its potential for alleviating rural poverty and unemployment, has thus been examined in the literature quite extensively in terms of its nature, magnitude, causal factors and impact on the household economy. The phenomenon in rural India at the macro level is characterised by an increase in the share of non-agricultural workforce engaged mainly in tertiary sector and having casual status. Theoretically, the changing occupational structure has come to be explained from two perspectives. First, from a developmental angle the changing workforce composition is attributed to factors like agricultural prosperity and growing urbanisation with their attendant positive linkages enabling labour force to diversify in order to tap the new income and employment opportunities. Diversification under such conditions is more a growth or prosperity-induced one. The second perspective is the distress kind where poverty, population growth and depleting resource base compel the labour force to diversify under duress, including resorting to seasonal migration to distant places. The empirical studies reviewed suggest that the phenomenon can be seen operating at both ends of the spectrum. In other words, the changing occupational structure in India is being influenced simultaneously by forces of development and distress. However, the extent of influence of these two forces is difficult to judge from the evidences provided by the existing studies given some of their limitations. The empirical studies, which focus on macro or regional level, relying only on secondary sources of data, have failed to capture the micro-level dynamics of diversification. On the other hand, those studies having a micro or village level focus by confining themselves mostly to a specific area are limited by their inability to relate the local labour processes to the broader context and change. It is here the need is felt for studies which cannot only explain the phenomenon in terms of its local nature and dynamics, but also provide a broader perspective that is a derivative of political, social and economic processes. In terms of broad basing the studies on diversification, another dimension which needs to be given attention is the relation between diversification, particularly of the distress type, and natural resources management. Even though the available evidence is very limited, distress diversification seems to be having clear links with changing natural resource base like degradation of forests. The studies suggest that improving the local resource base and its management can potentially reverse the trend of distress diversification.

As regards rural-urban migration, the studies reviewed suggest that to a large extent the widespread labour migration in India is explained more by structural factors like inequality in land ownership, poverty and agricultural backwardness than by models dealing purely with motivations of maximising the family's income and employment. Hence, rural-urban migration might help rural poor to overcome their problems of survival but may not lead to their real economic consolidation. Again, given the continued prevalence of distress migration, there is a need for studies that can help understand the phenomenon better, particularly for addressing policy initiatives aimed at reversing the trend of distress migration.

Having identified the major researchable issues concerning diversification and rural-urban migration, we now move on in the next two chapters, to examine the nature, causes and impact of diversification in the study villages.

3

OCCUPATIONAL DIVERSIFICATION IN TRIBAL VILLAGES

1. INTRODUCTION

The present Chapter deals with the nature of occupational diversification taking place in two tribal villages, viz Mahudi and Mahunala. Tribal villages are generally considered to be socio-economically homogeneous in nature with only a very little variation seen across different sections of the community. In recent decades the tribal communities across different parts of the country are experiencing many changes in their social and economic conditions including their identities due to their growing links with the outside systems (Sharma 1994).

The Chapter is organized in the following way. The condition of the natural resource base and the nature of occupational diversification that has occurred in Mahudi are dealt with in Section 2. Section 3 deals with the nature of occupational diversification in Mahunala. The factors determining the nature and extent of seasonal migration of households in the two villages are analyzed in Section 4. Section 5 draws a brief conclusion based on the analysis carried out in the Chapter.

2. OCCUPATIONAL DIVERSIFICATION IN MAHUDI

2.1 Resource Base of Mahudi

As mentioned in Chapter one, the village Mahudi has been studied in two phases. Though the difference in time period between the two phases is too short for any significant changes to occur on a long trajectory of livelihood transition, the major reason for a two phase study was to consolidate and build further on the learnings from the exploratory phase about the livelihood diversification. Before the findings of the two phases are discussed, a brief profile of Mahudi is presented below.

Mahudi is situated about 14 kms away from the taluka town, Jhalod, in the Dahod district. It falls in the semi-arid tropical area of Eastern Gujarat. The annual average rainfall in the region is about 989 mm. The rainfall is highly uncertain and also unevenly distributed across months. About 95 per cent of the rainfall is received during the monsoon from June to September, July being the rainiest month. The climate is hot and dry during summer and cool and humid during winter. The topography is a mixture of stony sloppy and plain lands having a significant bearing on cropping pattern and productivity. Except for five households of Vadi caste, the village is inhabited by the different clans of the Bhil tribe who are considered indigenous to the region. Of the 1,961 acres of total land, one-third is covered by the degraded forests which were quite dense a few decades ago, and about 60 per cent is cultivable land. The rest is accounted by the *gauchar* land, part of which has been utilised for various commercial and developmental purposes. All the tribal households own land with the average size being 2.46 acres. Only about 20 per cent of the cultivable land is irrigated with wells, river and canal. The population of the village has increased four-fold in about four and half decades. The total number of households which was 154 in 1951 increased to 528 in 1994. The total population increased from 883 to 3,470 during the same period indicating the growing pressure of the population and its impact on the carrying capacity of the land. While in 1951 every sq. km. of land area supported 129 persons, the same area in 1994 supported 436 persons leading to a drastic decline in the per capita availability of cultivable land. The household size increased from 5.8 to 6.6 during the same period. The literacy rate in 1994 was quite low with only 40 per cent among males and 19 per cent among females being literate.

2.2 Nature of Occupational Diversification in Mahudi: Insights from the Exploratory Phase

The following are the major observations about occupational diversification in Mahudi during 1993-94 as per the exploratory study:

Though agriculture remains a primary source of livelihood for almost all the households, bulk of them are supplementing their livelihood by diversifying into various other non-farm occupations (Table 3.1). One major way of diversification observed was seasonal migration of labour mainly to urban areas in Gujarat. About 76 per cent of the households were found resorting to seasonal migration. In about two-thirds of the migrating households even female members were found migrating indicating the gravity of the need for such diversification.

Besides about 22 per cent of the households were also found engaged in various non-farm occupations which are different from the highly casual and seasonal activities performed by the migrating households. These are mostly artisanal and service, trade and business activities, and regular white collar jobs under government or private sector. The households engaged in such non-farm occupations are mostly those who have some traditional or artisanal skills, or those who have certain level of educational qualification necessary for securing a regular job or able to mobilise resources to take up and pursue self-employment in trade and business. The households pursuing particularly trade and business as well as white collar jobs were found to be mainly from the upper echelons of the local community. In addition, most of the households were also found supplementing their livelihood through activities like animal husbandry and minor forest collection.

Table 3.1
Major Source of Livelihood/Occupation of the Sample Households and Composition of Labour Force in Mahudi (1993-94)

Livelihood/ Occupation	*Households*		*Labour Force*	
	No.	*Proportion (in %)*	*No.*	*Proportion (in %)*
Agriculture	311	98.4	1176*	97.7
Animal Husbandry	296	93.7	-	-
Wage Labour	261	82.6	617	51.2
(i) Migrant	240	76.0	531	44.1
(ii) Non-Migrant	21	6.6	86	7.1
Artisan/Services	28	8.9	-	-
Trade/Business	14	4.4	92**	7.6
White Collar/ Other Jobs	31	9.8	-	-
Total	316	-	1204	-

Source: Field Survey conducted in Mahudi Village, 1994.
NB : Because of the multiple occupations pursued by the households there is an overlap in the number of households and the labour force under different sources of livelihood.
* Includes labour force engaged in both Agriculture and Animal Husbandry.
** Includes labour force engaged in the last three livelihood sources.

In terms of the nature of the major sources of occupation, it could be seen that agriculture was being carried out mainly during two seasons, rainy season (kharif) and the winter season (rabi). The major crops grown during the rainy season are maize, paddy and pulses. The crops grown during winter are maize, wheat and chickpea.

Given the small size of landholding, family labour was found to be more than adequate to meet the labour requirements. Again, except for a small proportion, majority of the farmers were dependent on rainfall and winter moisture for raising crops. The household survey showed that almost 80 per cent of the village land was dependent on rainfall.

The adoption of modern agricultural technology consisting of high yielding variety (HYV) of crops and chemical fertilizers was only partial. Only wheat, grown during rabi season, was under HYV variety. Though most farmers used chemical fertilizers, the intensity of application was found to be low with the average consumption being about 46 kgs per farmer. As a result, crop yields were generally low with many farmers even feeling that there has been a decline in the yields over the years. The discussion with the farmers revealed that the yield per acre of maize was in the range of 350 to 450 kgs per acre. The smallholdings coupled with low yields resulted in inadequate food production for self-consumption. Even though many farmers sell wheat, pulses and even maize at times for cash but most of them were net buyers of foodgrains.

Maize which is the staple food, does not last for a full year. Hence, the households were compelled to buy maize during the lean months to supplement their own produce. Added to low production is the recurring drought during which the production from land goes down further and the food situation becomes even more precarious. Agriculture, thus is neither able to absorb fully the family labour nor able to meet fully the food requirements for most of the households. Even fodder from agriculture falls short of the need compelling many households to buy fodder to meet the shortage. None of the major interventions aimed at improving the situation of agriculture had made any significant impact. The modern technology comprising of HYV seeds and chemical fertilizers meant for improving the productivity had been adopted only partially. Even enabling farmers owning up to 7.5 acres of land to drought-proof their agriculture by providing free wells under a government scheme called, Jeevandhara, has not been able to make any significant impact. The wells are relatively shallow given the very low watertable and are unable to help farmers in getting adequate water to give them full protection against failure of rainfall. The government canal built to irrigate a part of the village land from a nearby dam also has failed to ensure adequate and assured water supply.

It is in this context, seasonal migration was found to be playing a significant role for a majority of the households. Seasonal migration has come to assume many unique features of its own. First of all, it is highly seasonal and cyclical in character. Bulk of the households (over 80 per cent) migrates mainly during winter and summer seasons though there are a few households who migrate during all the three seasons. The migration cycle starts soon after the harvesting of kharif crop and sowing of the rabi crop is over. The migration continues till the onset of the monsoon; however, the migrating households keep going back and forth between the village and the migration place for varying durations till they finally return with the arrival of rains.

In terms of labour force, on an average, about 2.2 persons in Mahudi migrated from each household. However, the actual number of migrants varied from one to five depending on the availability of surplus labour and the extent of need felt for supplementing the agricultural income. Female members also constituted a significant proportion of the total migrating labour force. In Mahudi, 39 per cent of the migrating labour force was female (Table 3.2). Young children also accompanied their mothers when they migrated.

Table 3.2
Distribution of Seasonal Migrant Labour by Nature of Work in Mahudi (1993-94)

(Figures in per cent)

Work	*Male*	*Female*	*Total*
Construction/Road Work	80.2	85.5	82.1 (436)
Factory Workers	6.8	3.4	5.5 (29)
Truck Loaders	4.6	0.0	2.8 (15)
Agricultural labour	7.1	8.2	7.6 (40)
Others	1.5	2.9	2.1 (11)
	100.0 (324)	100.0 (207)	100.0 (531)

Source: Field Survey conducted in Mahudi village, 1994.
Note: Figures in brackets are actual numbers.

The destination of migration is the prosperous rural and urban areas in central and southern Gujarat. Some of the major urban areas are Ahmedabad, Vadodara, Surat, Nadiad and Ankleshwar. Many migrate to more than one place during the year. This happens as some of the migrating people engage themselves in more than one occupation.

The seasonal migration which has become a major form of diversification in recent decades in the village was found to be largely due to distress conditions arising from degradation and decline of local resource base crucial for the livelihood of the households. The declining capacity of the local resources consisting primarily of land and forests coupled with increasing population pressure has compelled households to look for external avenues to supplement their livelihood. The agricultural land availability, a primary source of livelihood has declined over the years due to growing population pressure. The average size being about 2.5 acres, the land has been unable to meet fully the growing requirements of food, fodder, employment and cash income. With only a limited possibility of increasing agricultural yields through intensification, majority of the households have been forced to engage themselves in alternative sources of livelihood to supplement their small scale agriculture. At the same time, with the disappearance and degradation of forests, the households have been deprived of another vital source of their livelihood. Forests in the past had played a major role in meeting the households' requirements of food, fodder and fuelwood including providing employment and income. With the disappearance of rich forests mainly due to State sponsored forest extraction, the tribals who were left with no other local alternative to supplement their livelihood had to resort to seasonal migration to far-off prosperous areas of Gujarat. Simultaneously, the new economic growth that was taking place in the central and southern Gujarat by way of agricultural and industrial development and urbanisation with its growing demand for unskilled and casual labour provided a major opportunity for the tribals in the hinterlands like Dahod district to migrate and seek gainful employment to support their precarious livelihood. By being unskilled and semi-literate, they could mainly get employed as construction workers and agricultural labourers mostly on casual basis (Table 3.2). Despite being employed as lowly paid workers, the certainty of finding some job had made seasonal migration an attractive source of livelihood earning for a large number of tribals of this region.

During the exploratory study, it could also be observed that in one of the hamlets of the village an intervention in river water harvesting made by Sadguru Water and Development Foundation (SWDF), an NGO, had begun to show some positive results. The intervention had led to increased agricultural intensification which in turn had brought about some significant changes in the livelihood conditions of the households in terms of reduced dependence on seasonal migration. As a result, in the second phase study in Mahudi, we decided to focus mainly on assessing the impact of this intervention on the livelihood of these households in general and seasonal migration in particular.

2.3 Occupational Diversification in Mahudi: Insights from the Second Phase

The second phase of the study was conducted during 1996-2000 using various methods. Before looking at the diversification scenario as observed during the second phase in Mahudi, let us look at the conditions of some of the important resources. As compared to 1993-94, no major changes could be observed in the condition of the existing natural resources during the second phase. However, there were some attempts towards regenerating or harvesting some of the crucial resources having potential for improving the conditions of these resources in the years to come. In 1997, SWDF which helped in building a checkdam across the village river for harvesting water for agricultural purpose, took the initiative to organise Joint Forest Management (JFM) for regenerating the denuded forests in the village through people's participation. If implemented successfully, JFM has the potential to help the barren forests of Mahudi to regain their past glory. The JFM covers a forest area of 282 hectares with 368 households taking part in this endeavour of regenerating village forests. Besides regeneration of forests, there was a concerted attempt by a section of the village political leadership to bring irrigation to other parts of village not benefited by SWDF's intervention. The newly elected panchayat leaders of Mahudi had approached both the SWDF and government seeking help to harvest water for irrigation by tapping either a tank constructed in 1956 inside the forest area or the Machchan river by building another checkdam lift irrigation system. However, according to SWDF, since in both the cases the pipeline has to go through the area under the control of forest department, obtaining the permission for the purpose has proved to be a major hurdle. Much headway, hence, could not be made in this direction despite the interest shown by the new leadership which had even made bringing water to other parts of the village a major issue in the local village election.

The government under its fully subsidised scheme called Jeevandhara, continued to sanction wells to eligible farmers to provide life support to small farmers fully dependent on rainfed agriculture. Among the 45 households revisited in the second phase, three households were sanctioned Jeevandhara wells since 1994. A few households had tried unsuccessfully for Jeevandhara wells and a few more wanted to try in future. As noted earlier, majority of these Jeevandhara wells were unable to make any significant impact on the households in view of their shallowness and inadequate supply of water. By 1994, there were 36 such wells sanctioned in the village. With only a bleak prospect for tapping the ground water, hardly any new private investment was taking place in the village.

While the resource base largely remained the same, the population continued to grow putting pressure on the resource base. For the households surveyed in the second phase, the average households size increased from 7.7 in 1994 to 8.3 within a matter of about three and half years. The same land area now supports a higher population than during 1993-94.

The literacy level continued to be low; more so among the females. The prospects for higher education remained bleak with bulk of the school-going children dropping out by the time they completed secondary or high school. Only a few were able to complete high school and pursue higher education. The general tendency was one of discounting higher education among the households as there are only limited opportunities for securing regular jobs even with a higher educational qualification.

With the condition of the resource base, both human and physical, remaining largely same in the village, there were no major changes in the sources of livelihood and their nature. Small-scale rainfed agriculture supplemented by earnings from seasonal migration continued to be the dominant pattern of the livelihood for majority of the households in the village.

However, as compared to the overall village, the agricultural and livelihood situation in the intervention area of SWDF has been undergoing significant changes. The households coming under the intervention are able to irrigate their lands during winter and summer seasons. They are now able to raise an additional crop during summer. The availability of irrigation brought about an increase in cropping intensity and also changes in the cropping pattern.

The pulses are being replaced by cereals like maize and wheat during kharif and rabi. The green gram (Mung) is the additional crop being raised during summer. Because of irrigation, there is now an increased use of chemical fertilizers. As a result, the yields of crops, as reported by farmers, have now more than doubled as compared to the past. The increase in crop yields has brought about self-sufficiency in foodgrains and fodder among these households and most of them are able to sell their surplus foodgrains. The increase in the cropping intensity has increased the demand for labour, particularly for female labour for operations like sowing, weeding and harvesting.

Besides these changes, there are attempts by farmers to diversify their agriculture because of the improved resource base. A few enterprising and resourceful farmers are able to take up tomato growing in small plots of their lands. They have made huge investments and are also able to generate good income. Many farmers also have started growing vegetables and fruits, both for household consumption and for income generation purposes. Because of the encouragement from the NGO, the farmers in the intervention area also have taken up tree plantation mostly on their waste lands. Though eucalyptus is the major variety being grown, quite a few other varieties of trees also have been planted. The availability of water has enabled a good growth of tree plantations. The farmers now are able to meet their own wood and timber requirements besides supplementing their income through sale of trees. One more change we could see among these households is the increase in the livestock holding. The livestock maintenance by the households in Mahudi has been primarily for the purpose of supplementing agriculture in terms of draft power and manure. Now, because of increased availability of fodder and increased incomes, the households in the intervention area are able to acquire more livestock, draft as well as milch animals.

2.3.1 Seasonal Migration: The Trend Continues

As noted earlier, seasonal migration to prosperous urban and rural areas by the labour force was the major form of livelihood diversification that has taken place in Mahudi. This seasonal migration in the past two to three decades has become an important source of income and employment to the households in Mahudi. Except in the area where SWDF has made intervention, the findings of second phase from Mahudi reveal that the seasonal migration is continuing in the same magnitude and form. Almost all the households who reported seasonal migration as a source of livelihood during the exploratory phase continued with it. While in the non-intervention area over 80 per cent of the sample households still reported seasonal migration; it was about 73 per cent in the intervention area. In the case of non-intervention area a significant proportion (65 per cent) of migrant households reported migration by female members, as against only a small proportion (6.3 per cent) in the case of households in the intervention area. By nature, the migration continues to be highly seasonal and cyclical. Bulk of the households migrates mainly during two seasons, winter and summer. Some households migrate during all the three seasons, the proportion of such households being higher in non-intervention area (40 per cent) as compared to intervention area (20 per cent).

Another important aspect observed about the phenomenon is its ability to sustain itself by continuously getting replenished by new labour force. Even within a matter of about three and half years, we could observe in Mahudi that many old migrating people were being replaced by younger people who join the village labour force every year. In many of the households revisited, older people, both men and women, who were migrating earlier, had stopped migration and their role has been taken over by younger men and women from the family. This is how, probably, villages like Mahudi have become a constant source of informal labour force to cities and developed areas.

To capture some of the inner realities of occupational diversification in Mahudi, we carried out case study of two families representing two diverse scenarios. The first case study represents the dominant scenario where the households are compelled to migrate, while the second case represents a household which is able to overcome distress conditions and diversify locally.

The Compulsive Migrants: Dhira and Dala Brothers

Migration is a compulsory phenomenon for survival for most households in Mahudi. The households of Dhira Kalji and Dala Kalji exemplify in many ways the plight of such households in Mahudi. Dhira and Dala the two brothers who have got separated from the family live in one of the innermost hamlets of the village close to the degraded forests. They belong to Kamode clan whose members are considered low in the village social order. After family partition, both brothers inherited about 3-4 acres of undulating land each from their father, Kalji. The family of Dhira, the elder brother, lives in the old family house; Dala has still not been able to build a proper house. The household of Dhira consists of nine members including two daughters-in-law. Dala's family has seven members, the eldest child (son) being about 12 years old. Dala's wife has recently given birth to their (sixth) child. With the last son of Dhira recently discontinuing his schooling, none of Dhira's children is now educated beyond middle school. In Dala's household, none of the children in the school-going age have gone to school. Dala's household may remain illiterate even in the next generation, if the other younger children also do not go to school.

The families of Dhira and Dala are in third generation in the village with their grandfather having immigrated to Mahudi in search of cultivable land. The livelihood in the past though plagued by drought and robbery was largely dependent on the local resource base. Agriculture, livestock and forests were the main sources of livelihood especially during Kalji's time. Forests supplemented the livelihood in a major way. Besides hunting and gathering, forest development and harvesting provided good employment opportunities. The sudden depletion of forests deprived a major source of livelihood support. The resultant scarcity of fodder also reduced the significance of livestock over the years. The timber which was earlier easily available, free of cost now has to be bought from outside for meeting any domestic requirements.

Simultaneously, with the number of dependents increasing, the family had to look for alternative sources of income. Dhira and Dala started migrating seasonally to Baroda in search of unskilled construction work. After their marriage their wives also joined the migrant labour force. Lack of education and capital did not allow them to diversify into any other regular non-farm occupations. Agriculture remained in the same state without any major changes. Though they started using improved seeds and some chemical fertilizers, absence of irrigation despite some attempts to tap the local water tank, has made agriculture to remain in the low productivity state. A good harvest, as mentioned by Dhira's wife, has always been a source of happiness as it enables them to meet both their food and cash needs.

With the children of Dhira and Dala growing up, the division of the family became imminent. The family division further reduced the land and livestock availability at their disposal making seasonal migration to become a compulsive strategy for livelihood support. They also inherited and shared the debt of their father.

Dhira who is now in his mid 50s no longer migrates because of his age and health. The burden has now fallen on his sons and their wives. The family division not only affected the overall security but there are newer contingencies arising out of health and other compulsions. Dhira was forced to mortgage out an acre of land for Rs. 2000 to meet his medical expenses. For Dhira's first son, Raman, migration has become a year long activity both because of family debt and insufficient farm work. But now he migrates with his wife to Surat for two seasons, winter and summer. A skin allergy developed has now forced him to work only as a helper, thus reducing his earnings. Raman's brother, Parsing now works as a skilled construction worker earning about Rs. 150 per day. Raman and Parsing both return back to the village during peak agricultural operations and festivals.

The three migrating members in Dhira's household are able to bring substantial income. During 1996-97, the total net earnings after meeting the expenses at migration place amounted to about Rs. 30,000. The income from migration has become a major stabilising factor for meeting all the contingencies of the family. The earnings are used for buying additional foodgrains, fertilisers, seeds and other household needs. Repayment of loan and contributions to *chandlavidhi*[1] are also met out of the migration money. Dhira had incurred an expenditure of over Rs. 35,000 recently towards the marriage of Parsing, the bride price alone accounting for Rs. 30,000. While Dhira could raise about Rs. 10,000 through *Chandlavidhi,* he had to borrow another Rs. 15,000 pledging family jewellery. The rest came from migration and agriculture earnings. Dhira also conducted

1. *Chandlavidhi* is a ceremony held to solicit monetary contributions from relatives and friends to defray marriage and other expenses.

the marriage of one of his daughters. However, in this case much of the expenditure was met out of the bride price he received during the marriage.

Dhira got back recently the land he had pledged a few years back. He could also buy two milch cows. Dhira says, despite past difficulties he is now leading a contended life as his children are able to supplement the family's livelihood through migration. He is also confident that he would be able to repay the debt he has incurred towards Parsing's marriage. He is already thinking about his next son's marriage for which he needs to again mobilise a lot of money. With migration as a guaranteed source of income, there are no signs of worry. The forests nowhere figure in his present scheme of things.

For Dala, the partition of the family in a way worsened the situation. Unlike Dhira who has grown-up children to help him, Dala is struggling with the help of his wife to look after the family. Though Dala migrates seasonally, his wife is not able to accompany him regularly. Only once she could go with him. Regular pregnancies and child births have confined her only to household and agricultural work. Unfortunately the recent illness of Dala has forced them to mortgage bulk of their land for Rs. 3000 to meet both food and medical expenses. While education has been a luxury in such a situation for the children, the first son Kadiya, who is twelve years old has already been inducted into the labour force. Recently, he accompanied Dala for seasonal migration.

As food security and improving his house are the primary concern, Dala says, only hard work can help him which only means more of distress migration for his family.

Dhama's Diversified Way to Success

In a village where seasonal migration is the order for most households as a livelihood survival strategy, the path of diversified livelihood of Dhama Katchara stands as a glaring contrast. Even for once Dhama never faced any compulsion to resort to such a strategy. Dhama who is in his late 40s is an enterprising person belonging to Gharasia clan. The Gharasias are at the top of the Bhil social structure. The family of Dhama has always been at the forefront in capitalising economic opportunities. Dhama's father Katchara was quite well-off owning about twelve acres of land and plenty of livestock. With bountiful harvests and ample milk and ghee, the livelihood was well secured. Groundnut was the major cash crop grown. The family's resourcefulness had enabled Dhama to obtain decent education as he could study upto tenth standard, though his elder brother Rama remained illiterate.

Transporting timber was another major economic activity pursued by Dhama's father. They had four bullock carts. The bullock carts were being hired out to people trading in timber and bamboos. It was quite a lucrative activity. There were four hired labourers who were assisting the family in agriculture and transportation work. At the same time, Dhama's father was also buying bamboo from Rajasthan forests to sell them locally. The transportation business lasted till the forests got depleted. With multiple sources of earnings, the family's livelihood was well secured and self-sufficient. There existed no compulsion or desperation to incur any debt.

The exposure Dhama and Rama obtained while travelling with their father to neighbouring States for timber trade helped them when they grew up and got separated. Besides agriculture, they also picked up livestock trading. They would buy bullocks from places like Malwa in the neighbouring State and sell them for huge profits locally. At times, they would fatten young bullocks and sell them for profits. Rama pursued bullocks trading for about fifteen years. Tax and other restrictions forced him to give up inter-State trade of livestock. However, Dhama continued the activity of livestock trading locally, more as a commission agent. He goes to all local weekly markets and earns commission by helping the buyers and sellers to arrive at a deal. Rama and Dhama could earn substantially from livestock trade. Through the earnings from livestock business, Rama could meet the marriage expenses of his three sons. Dhama even refused the offers for bus conductorship and rural policeman of government, as his livestock business was much more lucrative than the salary he could have earned.

Dhama has at the same time tried to take advantage of many government schemes. He got a sprayer and a diesel engine for fifty per cent subsidy and fifty per cent loan under a government scheme. He was hiring out these equipments for rent. Dhama also wanted to get a free well sanctioned on his land. However, the spacing requirement between the existing wells came in the way of Dhama getting the well. Dhama, though is capable, is not interested in making investment in the well on his own as the ground watertable in the village is not high enough for such an investment.

Using his agricultural base and earnings from livestock business, Dhama has further diversified his activities. After building a pucca house in 1989, Dhama started grocery and grains business which has got further expanded recently. At the same time, he has been capitalising on any windfall opportunity which has come his way. Once, he had mobilised labourers on commission basis for making arrangements for a public function in Baroda. Yet another time, through poultry business he could make additional income. Recently again on a commission basis, he could earn Rs. 22,000 by selling tiles which emboldened him to think in terms of starting trade in building materials. He also has a plan to start a flour mill as he feels there is enough demand for it.

While diversification strategy continues with success, Dhama has at the same time given similar attention to his family's welfare and advancement. All his four children including his two daughters have obtained decent education. Whenever he has earned surplus profit, he has saved a part of it in the name of his children for their future needs.

Recently, Dhama renovated his house at the cost of Rs. 65,000 mobilised through his own earnings and taking a loan from a money-lender by pledging the silver jewellery inherited from his mother.

Dhama, who has realised the ill-effects of the Bhil practice of bride price, says he will not take bride price for his daughters though he may pay for his sons.

The above two cases clearly indicate that the socio-economic base of a household plays a major role in determining the nature of diversification. The case of Dhama though is worth replicating but not many households in Mahudi have a similar socio-economic base to diversify on a strong footing. The dominant reality, unfortunately, is that of Dhira and Dala wherein the households adopt distress migration as a compulsive strategy without much scope for any consolidation and advancement.

3. OCCUPATIONAL DIVERSIFICATION IN MAHUNALA

The village Mahunala has been selected mainly to broaden, in the district, our understanding of the phenomenon of diversification as observed in village Mahudi. The type of diversification observed in Mahudi is prevalent widely in most of the villages in the district. The talukas of Limkheda and Jhalod in which Mahunala and Mahudi are located are adjacent to each other and have broadly similar agro-climatic environment. In this section, we make an attempt to capture the major characteristics of the resource base of Mahunala and the nature of the occupational diversification in comparison to village Mahudi.

3.1 Resource Base of Mahunala

Mahunala is situated about 17 kms from the taluka headquarters, Limkheda, and is on the road connecting Limkheda and Dhanpur. From the connecting main road, the village is about 4 kms interior. With the recent metalling of the interior road, Mahunala is now connected by a pucca road to the district and the taluka headquarters.

Like Mahudi, Mahunala is also inhabited by the Bhils who are considered indigenous to the region. The Bhil population in Mahunala is divided into sixteen exogamous clans with Tadvi, Medha, Ninama, Hathila and Bamaniya being the major ones.

Mahunala belongs to a Group Panchayat with headquarters of the Panchayat located in the neighbouring Bor village. However, the Sarpanch (elected head of the Pachayat) is from Mahunala represented by a woman. The village also has been recently electrified with a few households having power connections for domestic use.

The total land area of Mahunala is 763.7 acres (Table 3.3). Out of which, about 41.2 per cent (314.6 acres) is accounted by cultivable land which is the major resource base of the households in the village. The forest area occupies about 38.8 per cent of the total area. The rest 20 per cent land area is accounted by land classified as cultivable waste which also includes *gauchar* and groves.

Table 3.3
Land Classification of Mahunala (1991)

Sr. No.	*Land Type*	*Area (in acres)*	*% to total*
1.	Cultivable land	314.58	41.19
2.	Cultivable waste (including *gauchar* and groves)	152.88	20.02
3.	Forest	296.27	38.79
	Total	763.73	100.0

Source: District Census Hand Book, 1991, Panchmahal District.

The cultivable land which is owned by the households is highly undulating in nature with a mixture of stony, sloppy and plain lands. A PRA exercise carried out by

KRIBP, an NGO working in the village, in 1993 revealed that plain lands which are suitable for cultivation of paddy accounts for only about 10 per cent of the cultivable area. All the households in the village own some land. The average ownership of cultivable land comes to about 1.74 acres which indicates prevalence of an adverse land-man ratio similar to that of Mahudi. The discussion with the households revealed that quite a few households have augmented their land availability by encroaching land coming under the forest area. The encroachment has taken place over the past few decades. The households who have encroached forestland are hopeful of getting their encroachments regularised. At the same time, part of the *gauchar* land in the village also has been encroached by the households.

The construction of an irrigation dam downstream of the river Hadaf which passes through Mahunala also has affected the availability of cultivable land in the village. During the rainy season the backwaters of the dam submerge part of the lands of Mahunala falling along the river. The farmers who own land in the submerged area are unable to cultivate their lands. However, during winter when the river water recedes, these households cultivate their lands. Those households whose lands and homestead, partly or fully, have got submerged have been monetarily compensated by the government. Though we could not gather information about the total area affected by seasonal submergence, the sample survey carried out revealed that nearly 20 per cent of the land owned by farmers was affected. The construction of dam at the same time seems to have affected positively the ground watertable in the village enabling farmers in the vicinity of backwaters to tap ground water for irrigating their lands.

Forests: The forest area which accounts for about 39 per cent of the total area comes under the forest department. The story of forests of Mahunala is almost similar to that of forests of Mahudi. Presently, the forests depict a picture of total depletion that has taken place over the years. As recalled by people, forests of Mahunala were quite dense about three decades ago with diverse flora and fauna. The people were dependent on forests for livelihood in a major way. The forests were an important source of food, fodder, fuelwood, timber and even employment. They played a major role in enriching the micro-environment. The dense forests, however, disappeared rapidly depriving people a key source of livelihood. One of the major reasons responsible for depletion was the clearing of forests for commercial purpose by private contractors and a forest labour co-operative with the approval of the government. The forests since then have failed to regenerate on their own. Coupled with the commercial harvesting, the local people also have encroached forest land for cultivation resulting in the decline of actual area under forests. Presently people depend on forests for fodder and for fuelwood only. The KRIBP has also initiated, since 1997, JFM in a small area (10 hectares) of forest land in Mahunala. There has been some resentment and opposition to the initiative from a section of the village households who fear JFM may lead to confiscation of their encroached land. However, despite the opposition, KRIBP has gone ahead with the implementation of JFM by taking the co-operation of other households. Depending upon the success of the present experiment, JFM will be expanded further to cover more forest land in the village.

Water Resources: The Hadaf river, small streams and wells are the three major sources of water used for domestic and agricultural purposes in Mahunala. Using pumpset and pipes, the villagers lift water to irrigate their fields particularly during winter. Many households own wells built either with own capital or with the assistance of some government schemes like Jeevandhara. As per the sample survey, about fifty per cent of the households owned either a pucca or a katcha well. In many cases these wells are shared by more than one household. The panchayat has installed a few handpumps for meeting the drinking water needs. In one of the hamlets (Khobra faliya) recently KRIBP has built a small checkdam which can irrigate about 20-25 acres of land. KRIBP has also helped about nine households to renovate their wells. The practice of selling water prevails in the village. The well owners sell water during winter at the rates varying from Rs. 30 to Rs. 70 per hour. Besides, the practice of hiring out pumpset and pipes to those who lift water from stream or river is also widely prevalent.

Demographic Profile: The recent demographic changes of Mahunala give a picture of a steady population growth leading to increased pressure on the resource base. As per the census data, the total population of Mahunala which was 641 in 1971 has increased to 1045 by 1991. An estimate made by us shows that the population of Mahunala in 1997 was about 1358. This estimate is based on the total number of households (181) enumerated during the PRA exercise carried out by KRIBP and the average household size (7.5) as arrived at by the sample survey carried out during 1997 (Table 3.4).

Table 3.4
Demographic Profile of Mahunala, 1971-1997

Sr. No.	*Details*	*1971*	*1981*	*1991*	*1997*
1.	Total population	641	822	1045	1358
	Male	356	426	538	-
	Female	285	396	507	-
2.	Households	100	117	122	181
3.	Household size	6.4	7.02	8.6	7.5
4.	Sex ratio	800	930	942	923
5.	Literacy rate (%)				
	Male	19.4	7.8	19.5	35.9
	Female	Neg	Neg	4.7	18.1
6.	Density (Per Sq. Km.)	207	266	338	439

Source: 1. Respective year's District Census Handbooks for 1971, 1981 and 1991.
2. The 1997 figures are based on the PRA Enumeration of households done by KRIBP and a sample survey (n=20) carried out by the authors.
3. Neg. = Negligible.

The population thus has more than doubled in a period of about two and half decades. The number of households has risen from 100 in 1971 to about 181 by 1997. The density of population has more than doubled during the same period. The demographic changes noticeable in Mahunala are thus very similar to the one observed in the case of Mahudi. Even the scenario with regard to literacy is similar between the two villages. Though there is an improvement in the male literacy during the period of analysis, the female literacy level remains abysmally low. As per the sample survey of 1997, while the male literacy rate in Mahunala was about 36 per cent; the female literacy stood at about 18 per cent.

The population being Bhils, the settlement pattern of households in Mahunala is similar to one noticeable in Mahudi. The households are scattered all over the cultivable land area in the village. Broadly, the villagers identify about five settlement clusters or hamlets viz., Khobra faliya, Patel faliya, Katiya faliya, Hanuman faliya and Nishal faliya. These hamlets have been named after either a dominant clan which inhabits the hamlet or a landmark in the hamlet like a temple or a school. Each household is a homestead with the house being located at an elevated place of the farm land. In most cases houses are surrounded by vegetable gardens and trees.

Household Assets: The households of Mahunala own varied assets which support their livelihoods. Land is the primary asset of all the households. In two ways the ownership of land becomes important for the Bhils. Besides being a source of food and fodder, ownership of land helps them in securing a self-image of being peasants. Such an identity assumes added significance in the context of the growing tendency of the community to look outwards for securing livelihood particularly as migrant labourers.

Though there are variations across households, the average size of ownership of land is very low (1.74 acres).

Quite a few households mortgage out their lands, in full or part, for raising debt to meet family contingencies like marriage and medical expenses. Similarly, many households use their silver jewellery for raising debt from private sources. Owning of silver jewellery is a custom among Bhils.

Trees on bunds and wastelands are other assets of value. Though eucalyptus is the commonly found tree species, a large variety of other trees can be seen on farmers' fields such as mango, bamboo, mahuda, neem, bor, tamarind, etc. Besides meeting fuelwood, timber, fruits and fodder needs, trees also help in generating some cash income. KRIBP is encouraging tree growing by farmers. It has helped set up four nurseries by farmers in the village with the help of the forest department. Saplings of a wide variety of trees are distributed to farmers.

Livestock are another important productive assets of the households. The livestock owned include bullocks, cows, buffaloes, goats and poultry birds. Most of the households keep bullocks followed by buffaloes, cows and goats. The bullocks are used basically as draft animals. Buffaloes and cows are maintained for meeting domestic milk needs. The goats and poultry birds are reared for generating cash income through sale. The dung from animals is used for meeting the needs of manure and fuel. The animals thus are an important complementary assets of livelihood.

3.2 Occupational Diversification in Mahunala

Overall, the condition of Mahunala is characterised by growing population and depleting resources resulting in an adverse land-man ratio. Given such a resource context, the present section tries to examine the nature of occupational structure prevailing in Mahunala.

Table 3.5 depicts the broad occupational structure of Mahunala. Since land is owned by all households, agriculture is pursued by all the households. Besides agriculture, the households supplement their livelihood through other sources. About 75 to 80 per cent of them migrate seasonally to better-off areas in search of employment. About a fifth of the households pursue, both within and outside the village, various non-farm occupations like trade and business, carpentry and white collar government jobs. These non-farm occupations are mostly those which require some special skill or educational qualification or capital investment by the households.

Table 3.5
The Broad Occupational Structure of Mahunala (1997)

Occupations	*Proportion of Households Pursuing (%)*
1. Agriculture	100
2. Seasonal Migration	75 - 80
3. Non-farm Occupations	15 - 20

Source: Based on the Sample Survey (n=20) and PRA exercise carried out by KRIBP. Proportion by range is given for occupations 2 and 3 as revealed by the PRA data. Due to overlap of occupations, the figures do not add up to hundred.

Apart from these three sources, many households were found supplementing their livelihood through numerous other sources of income and employment. These included money lending, sale of water for irrigation, hiring out irrigation equipments, collection and sale of minor forest products, and wage employment under a government programme or on private farms. Though most of these activities are pursued by only a small number of households, but still they serve as an important supplementary source of livelihood for these households.

Overall, though agriculture remains the primary occupation, the households in Mahunala have diversified into many other occupations. The major form of diversification is the seasonal migration which makes households to depend on external avenues for sustaining their livelihood. We look at now the nature of the two major sources of livelihood in Mahunala viz. agriculture and seasonal migration to understand their significance for the households.

Agriculture

Agriculture is carried out mainly in two seasons, rainy season (kharif) and winter season (rabi). The major crops grown during rainy season are maize, paddy and pulses which are mixed with maize. The crops grown during winter are maize, wheat and chickpea. Wheat grown during winter is the only crop under high yielding variety. The dependence on rainfall and the associated risk is the primary reason for the prominent use of local varieties of seeds. KRIBP has been trying to disseminate improved varieties of maize and paddy using participatory technology development approach in a part of the village. Agriculture is carried out using mostly family labour. However, limited hiring of labour for operations like weeding and harvesting is prevalent among the households. Recently, some farmers are hiring tractors for operations like ploughing. Most farmers use chemical fertilizers for enhancing productivity. However, with an average per acre use of about 26 kgs, the intensity of fertilizer application is low. Those with well, irrigate their lands for winter crops. Some of the farmers buy water from their neighbours. Given the dependence of agriculture on rainfall and due to low adoption of yield enhancing techniques, the yields of crops are found to be generally low. For maize which is the staple crop, the yields were found to be in the range of 350-450 kgs per acre. While much of the agricultural produce is used for self-consumption; farmers sell part of their produce, particularly pulses and wheat for meeting their cash needs. As a result of low yield and small holdings, not many households are able to meet their food requirements fully from land. Agriculture is also not able to absorb the labour force fully throughout the year. It is in this context, diversification for supplementing the livelihood from agriculture has assumed importance.

Seasonal Migration

Like in Mahudi, seasonal migration is the key diversification strategy adopted by households in Mahunala to overcome the constraints imposed by agriculture. The phenomenon which started over three decades ago, has come to play a significant role for majority of the households for sustaining their livelihood. As revealed by the sample survey and the PRA exercise, over 75 per cent of the households resort to seasonal migration. This magnitude is almost similar to the magnitude of seasonal migration observed in Mahudi. In about 80 per cent of the migrating households (60 per cent of the total) even female members migrate. In terms of labour force, on an average about 2.3 persons migrate from each household. However, the actual number of migrants varies from one to five depending on the availability of surplus labour and the intensity of the need felt for supplementing agricultural income. About 45 per cent of the migrating labour force is constituted by female labour. The extent of participation of female labour in migration is an indication of the gravity of the need felt by households to migrate.

The migration of households in Mahunala is highly seasonal in nature and having a cyclical form. The migration starts mainly after the harvesting of kharif crop and sowing for winter has been completed. The migrants return for winter (rabi) harvest and Holi festival. With the completion of the festival and marriages, the members migrate again during the summer only to return on the onset of rains for starting a new season.

Most of the households (about 80 per cent) migrate for two seasons (winter and summer). While migrating for two seasons is the general pattern, there are a few households who migrate during all the three seasons. The availability of excess labour or the compulsion to earn additional income is the major factor influencing the number of seasons a household migrates or even the duration of migration. In terms of duration or actual days of migration, there are wide variations. The number of days of migration for a male labour, as per the sample survey, varies from 45 to 270 days with an average of 175 days. A female labour migrates for 30 to 270 days with an average of 143 days. Overall, the total person days of migration for a household vary from 30 to 915 days with the average being 374 days. During migration, it is common to observe the members returning home intermittently to remit their earnings and take a short break from the tedious work.

In terms of destinations, the labourers migrate to prosperous areas in central and southern Gujarat. Some of the major places include rural and urban areas of Ahmedabad district, Vadodara district, Kheda district and cities like Surat and Ankleshwar. Many (nearly one-third) migrate to more than one place during the year. This happens as these migrating people engage themselves in more than one occupation like construction and agriculture during migration. For example, during winter, members of a household may go to a village in Kheda district for agricultural work. The same members during summer would go to Ahmedabad for construction work. The parents in most cases (two-third) take with them young children when they migrate. At times, the grown-up children help their parents in their work. Most of the people during migration live in open places, both in the cities and villages braving cold, heat and rains with total absence of any basic amenities. A few get to live in worksheds or rooms provided by the employers.

The activities pursued by migrants are largely similar to that of the migrants from Mahudi. Construction is the major activity in which both male and female migrant labourers are involved (Table 3.6). Agricultural labour is the next important activity overall. At the same time, a significant proportion of migrants are involved in both construction and agricultural labour work. Besides construction and agriculture, some of them work in cities as unskilled factory workers or as watchmen. Under construction activity, the migrants perform variety of unskilled work like carrying load and digging. Only a very few who are skilled, work as masons. Under agriculture, the migrants are involved mainly in the harvesting activity.

Table 3.6
Activities Pursued under Seasonal Migration

Sr. No.	*Activities*	*No. of Workers*	*Male*	*Female*
1.	Construction	15	8	7
2.	Agriculture labour	5	2	3
3.	Construction plus Agriculture labour	11	7	4
4.	Factory work/Watchmen	4	2	2
	Total	35	19	16

Source: Sample Survey in Mahunala.

The earnings from migration vary widely across households. The major determining factors of earnings by a household are the number of family members migrating and the total duration for migration. As per the sample survey, the gross earnings for the sample households during 1997-98 varied from Rs. 1300 to Rs. 29,000 with an average earning of Rs. 14,446. In the average earnings, the contribution of the female labourers accounted for about 40 per cent. The net inflow of remittances from the gross earnings varied from Rs. 1000 to Rs. 18,300 for the sample households. The average annual net inflow for a household was of the order of Rs. 9,483.

The seasonal migration as can be discerned from the above analysis has thus become a major source of livelihood for the households of Mahunala. It is contributing quite significantly both to the employment and the income of the migrating households. The households as a result have come to depend on seasonal migration as an assured means for supplementing their livelihood from agriculture (see Box 3.1).

Box 3.1

Survival and Consolidation: The Case of Motibhai

The household of Motibhai Virabhai Bamaniya (about 50 years of age) in Mahunala is a typical case of how seasonal migration can play a crucial cushioning role in the survival strategy of a household. The household of Motibhai consists of 13 members. After partition of land with his brothers, Motibhai inherited about 1.5 to 2 acres of land in two parcels. Motibhai belongs to Bamaniya clan considered low in the village social order. In Mahunala, Motibhai's family is now in the third generation. Motibhai's grandfather came to Mahunala looking for a job as a herdsman on the invitation from a relative. Subsequently, he bought some land in the village from a person willing to dispose of his land.

Motibhai's father, Virabhai inherited about 5 acres of land from Motibhai's grandfather. Agriculture was then the major occupation. A number of animals were kept both for complementing and supplementing agriculture. Virabhai had about 5-6 cows, 4 buffaloes, and over 40 goats. Virabhai never had to leave Mahunala for supplementing his livelihood. There were also flourishing forests with fruits, honey, fodder and timber available in abundance. Motibhai, when he was young, worked as a labourer in a Forest Labour Co-operative promoted for harvesting timber and charcoal making. Once the forests were denuded and ceased to be a means of sustenance, migration became an alternative avenue for supplementing livelihood. Motibhai started migrating to Baroda for construction work. Despite owning land, his family did not have enough food, as the yields were very low. Motibhai continued his migration till his sons started migration about 15 years ago.

None of the children of Motibhai are literate. All the three sons now migrate. The first two sons, Bachu and Balwant Singh migrate with their wives and children to Baroda. Bachu works as a watchman for a building contractor throughout the year. He earns a monthly salary of Rs. 1,200. The other migrating members of the family including two female members work as casual construction labourers. They return home during peak agricultural season and also attend festivals and marriages. All the five migrating members earn overall about Rs. 29,000 during a year (1997-98). After meeting their expenses, they remit about Rs.18,000 back home. The earnings from migration thus are much higher than the annual earnings from 1.5 acre of family land. The family, because of earnings from migration, has ensured its food security. At the same time, the surplus labour of the family has been absorbed gainfully outside agriculture. As Motibhai puts it, 'our agriculture is only *Aat dini kheti'* (Eight-days farming). The agriculture throughout the year generates about 120 person days of employment. Mostly, Motibhai and his wife work on their farming, though they employ some labour for operations like weeding and harvesting. His sons come back and help during peak operations.

Besides ensuring food safety and employment, migration has become an avenue for social and economic consolidation of the family. The earnings in the past had helped to meet his two sons' marriage expenses. Motibhai had paid a bride-price of Rs. 5,000 and Rs. 10,000 for the marriage of his first and second son respectively. His third son, Kalio, in fact, is saving on his own from the earnings of migration to meet his marriage expenses. Motibhai claimed that he contributed about Rs. 10,000 to *Chandlavidhi* annually. The contributions, in a sense are an investment as those who receive his contributions would repay double the amount when Motibhai holds the *vidhi*. Recently Motibhai bought a bullock for Rs. 5,000 mobilised out of the remittances. He has a plan to deepen and renovate an old well on his field. The well-deepening would require about Rs. 10,000. Motibhai is confident of mobilising the sum from the earnings of his three migrating sons. Apparently contended, Motibhai intends to send his grandson for schooling in the village.

4. DETERMINANTS OF SEASONAL MIGRATION

The continued prevalence of seasonal migration in villages like Mahudi and Mahunala on a large scale is the result of various socio-economic factors operating in a mutual reinforcing way on these households. The factors which initially triggered off migration not only remain still valid but have been further strengthened by developments occurring subsequently.

Before we identify the common factors compelling households in Mahudi and Mahunala to migrate, first we make an attempt in this section to analyze the utilization pattern of remittances from migration. The analysis of utilization pattern would give an indication about possible household level factors influencing seasonal migration.

4.1 Utilisation Pattern of Remittances

During the repeat survey in Mahudi, an attempt was made to find out the major items on which the migrant households spend their earnings. Table 3.7 presents the utilization pattern of remittances separately for households coming under intervention and non-intervention areas in Mahudi. Given the changed economic conditions in the intervention area, it was decided to look at the pattern separately for these two groups of migrant households.

Table 3.7
Utilisation Pattern of Remittances in Mahudi (1996-97)

Major Purposes	*Number of Migrant Households*	
	Non-Intervention Area	*Intervention Area*
Consumption	13	2
Seasonal Production	17	11
Livestock	3	4
Housing	4	2
Land Mortgaging	8	3
Bride-Price	10	6
Chandla	8	6
Health	5	1
Loan Repayment	10	3

Source: Based on a Sample Survey of 36 migrant households in Mahudi in 1997. Because of the appearance of a household under multiple purposes, the frequencies do not add up to the total sample.

The needs of the migrant households are quite diverse. The earnings from migration get utilized for a wide variety of purposes depending on household compulsions. The purposes of utilization in both the areas range from food for basic survival to meeting certain social obligations to investing for economic consolidation. However, there are certain differences in the pattern of spending between the two areas. In non-intervention area, food is the primary purpose is evident from the fact that out of 20 migrants surveyed, 13 reported utilizing their earnings for buying food and other essential items of consumption. In the intervention area, because of the improved food security only 2 out of 16 migrant households spend their earnings on food. Meeting the expenses on agricultural inputs like seed and fertilizers is another major purpose in both the areas. 17 out of 20 migrants in non-intervention area and 11 out of 16 migrant households reported spending on seasonal production. In an indirect way, spending on seasonal production ensures food security for the households. In the intervention area, due to increased agricultural intensity households reported increased spending on farm inputs like water and fertilizers. In the intervention area, the reduced spending on food is now being utilized for augmenting agricultural production.

The migrant households also utilize their earnings to augment production resources. This includes buying livestock and mortgaging-in land. A few households, 3 in non-intervention area and 4 in intervention area, reported utilizing their earnings for buying bullocks or goats or buffaloes. Similarly, 8 households in non-intervention area and 3 in intervention area reported that by utilizing the surplus from migration, they have taken land of borrower households on mortgage, in the process expanding their own production base. Some of the households, in both the areas, reported spending on medical expenses and for house renovation or construction. Both these purposes are meant for securing family's health and well-being.

Meeting food needs and augmenting production base apart, a significant number of migrant households spend their earnings to meet the expenses of certain social customs like bride-price and *chandlavidhi.* 10 households in non-intervention area and 6 in intervention area reported utilizing earnings for paying bride-price. Similarly, 8 households in non-intervention area and 6 in intervention area reported making contribution to *chandlavidhi* from the migration income.

Many households, particularly in non-intervention area, despite their earnings from migration borrow money frequently to meet various contingencies. The migration income becomes a source for repaying the loans borrowed from different sources. 10 of the 20 migrant households in non-intervention area have diverted their earnings for repaying loans. The number of households who utilized their remittances to repay their loans was found to be much lower (3) in the intervention area. This could be because of the improved economic situation which seems to have made them financially independent.

Before drawing any inference based on the above analysis, it must be mentioned that though there are variations between the two areas, the pattern of utilization prevailing in the non-intervention area represents the dominant pattern in Mahudi. Because, as compared to the intervention area the non-intervention area constitutes the major segment (88 per cent) of the village population.

Considering the pattern in the non-intervention area, it becomes clear that ensuring food security, directly or indirectly becomes the primary purpose of earnings from migration. Utilising the earnings for purposes like buying food and agricultural inputs are meant for ensuring such security. In a way, this is substantiated by only a small number of households in the intervention area utilizing their earnings for such purposes. At the same time, a few households, particularly, those who earn relatively a higher income from migration, are able to divert part of their earnings for economic consolidation of the family. These households invest in buying assets, lending money and renovating their houses. Economic purposes apart, social obligations of the households are the other major channels for utilizing the migration money.

4.2 Factors Influencing Seasonal Migration

Based on the above analysis of utilization pattern and the

nature of diversification in Mahudi and Mahunala, we are able to identify the following reasons as the major factors influencing the nature and magnitude of seasonal migration.

(i) Declining Land Availability and Agricultural Surplus

Though all the households own land, the extent of land owned is so low that it is unable to support fully the growing needs of the households. With a steady growth in the population, the average land availability is continuously declining putting the households under further stress. Coupled with small sized land, there are other constraints imposed like continued dependence on the rainfall and lack of spread of modern agricultural technology. Hence, the yields of crops are found to be low. For maize which is the staple crop, the yields were found to be in the range of 350-450 kgs per acre. As a result, the households are unable to meet their food requirement fully. Though they sell some of the agricultural produce like pulses and wheat, they are net buyers of food, mainly maize which is the staple food. For a large number of households, supplementary sources of income become essential to meet the food requirements even during a normal rainfall in a year. At the same time, there is a need for cash income to meet other household essentials like sugar, salt, vegetables, edible oil, medicine and clothes. Further, there are other important inputs like seeds, fertilizers and fodder which also need to be bought. Some of the households try to supplement their agricultural income through collection and sale of minor forest produce, sale of trees, and sale of goats and poultry birds. But still they cannot meet fully all their essential requirements. There is thus a compelling reason for most of the households to earn additional income from other sources. During the drought years, the compulsion is even greater. It is here that the forests are missed greatly by these households. The forests in the past were greatly supplementing the livelihood in meeting many basic requirements. With the forests disappearing and the agriculture unable to meet fully all their essential needs, most households are compelled to migrate.

(ii) Growing Population Pressure and Surplus Labour

The problem arising out of the limited availability of the land is further compounded by growing population pressure. The growing population has led to mainly two kinds of negative impacts on the households. As a result of rapid population growth there is growing partition of families leading to fragmentation of land holdings. The per capita land availability is declining drastically resulting in land being unable to meet fully the basic food requirement. Secondly, growing population and declining land availability have generated the problem of surplus labour. Due to the small size of land coupled with low cropping intensity, there is only a limited scope for absorption of the family labour throughout the year. Bulk of the available family labour is rendered idle as a result. With only a very limited scope or opportunity for absorption of the surplus labour locally, either in the farm or non-farm sector, seasonal migration has been found to be the only alternative for gainful employment. Higher the surplus labour, the higher is the consequent number of migrants per household.

(iii) Economic Compulsion of Social Obligations

Apart from the need to meet the subsistence requirements, the Bhils have certain other equally compelling social obligations for which they need substantial cash income. Given the limited earnings from land, migration is seen as the only potential way by which both types of needs of the households can be met. The Bhils have in vogue two widely prevalent social practices or customs which impose a major economic burden. One is the practice of bride-price and another is the *chandlavidhi*. Though both the practices have evolved as a mutual insurance measure against certain social risks faced by the households, in reality they have turned out to be issues of social prestige and economic burden. The bride-price is the system of paying a pre-determined money at the time of the marriage by the groom's father in return for the girl to the bride's father. The bride-price is used by the girl's father for meeting marriage expenses and for buying silver ornaments for the girl. The surplus, if any, is utilised for meeting other obligations of the family. The amount of bride-price to be paid varies according to the social and economic status of the bride's family. The bride-price could be as high as even Rs. 30,000 which in most cases, is manifold higher than the annual income from the land. In addition to paying the bride price, the groom's family also incurs substantial expenditure on the marriage. The money for the bride-price and the marriage expenses are raised by the households from various sources such as agriculture, loan from moneylenders or relatives, organising a *chandlavidhi* and accumulated savings from the earnings of migration. In case of taking a big loan for bride-price, the burden of repaying the principal and interest necessitates increased migration by the family members including the newly wed girls. In many cases, in order to reduce the future burden of loan, male members migrate and save as much as possible from the earnings even before the marriage.

During the time of marriage, it is common for a Bhil household to organise a function called *chandlavidhi* in which relatives and friends come and make monetary contributions in order to enable the household to mobilise part of the funds required to meet the marriage expenses. Though evolved as a social security mechanism for the benefit of families faced with such contingencies, *chandlavidhi* at the same time imposes a burden on both the recipient and the contributor. For the recipient household, it becomes a kind of an obligation as the monetary contributions received have to be reciprocated compulsorily. In reciprocation, the household has to pay one and half times or double the amount received whenever the contributors hold similar *vidhi*. At the same time, the households apart from reciprocating, are morally bound to contribute as per their capacity, whenever invited for a *chandlavidhi*. Many take pride in making higher contributions as some social prestige is attached to it. *Chandlavidhi* is also organised during other occasions like house construction and starting a new venture. Most households incur a significant expenditure on account of *chandlavidhi* annually. Earnings from migration play a crucial role in meeting the expenses of these social compulsions.

(iv) Economic Consolidation and Risk Reduction

While for most households, migration is an indispensable supplementary avenue to meet the basic livelihood requirements, for quite a few it is also seen as a source for strengthening and consolidating the household's economic position. The surplus earnings over and above what is required to meet the subsistence needs are utilised for improving the asset base of the household. This takes place in various forms. The livestock, particularly draft animals, play a crucial role in supporting the agriculture. There is a need to replenish the livestock as and when there is depletion (see Box 3.1). Many households invest their earnings from migration in buying bullocks and cows. The renovation of old house is another purpose for which many utilise their earnings. Many households also invest in buying silver jewellery which can be used as a collateral for taking loans in times of need.

At the same time, some households utilise the income from migration for expansionary and investment activities. These include mortgaging-in land and lending money at high interest rates. The mortgaging of land helps these households in two ways. First, the households by taking the land on mortgage are able to augment their limited land base to meet their food needs. Second, they are able to generate some surplus as the prevailing terms of mortgaging are normally found in their favour. Money-lending is another activity for these households to invest their income. By lending to the needy at rates ranging from 24 to 100 per cent per annum, they are able to earn attractive returns. Investments of these kinds are mostly made by households with surplus earnings from migration. Overall, these investments are aimed at economic consolidation and increasing the household's ability to face many risks. Seasonal migration is seen by these households as a means for consolidating their economic position.

(v) Limited Employment Opportunities

The growing dependence of the labour force on seasonal migration is also attributable to the limited employment opportunities available locally both in the farm and non-farm sectors. As discussed earlier, the small scale agriculture with its low cropping intensity is unable to absorb the surplus labour force fully. In most cases, the family labour is found more than adequate for farm operations. Even in cases where labour is hired for agricultural operations, it is only for very limited operations and period. Further, there are households pursuing various types of non-farm occupations, other than those pursued under seasonal migration, both within and outside the village (see Box 3.2). However, there is only a limited scope for large scale absorption of labour force under these activities. The reasons are manifold: lack of necessary skill and capital among households to pursue non-farm occupations; limited growth potential of non-farm activities due to limited local demand; and limited job opportunities under government sector even for those possessing educational qualifications. Further, the local regional economy being backward industrially and in terms of infrastructure, there is only a limited scope for a rapid growth of various employment opportunities to absorb this type of rural labour force.

Box 3.2
Migrants Turned Entrepreneurs: The Case of Navalsingh and his Wife

Although seasonal migration generates much needed income, for a migrant there is always a desire that one day some alternative to migration is thrown up and the need for migrating under compulsion does not arise. The harsh conditions of living and working experienced during migration are the cause for such dejection. The case of Navalsingh Tadvi (30 years old), an educated and an enterprising trader of Mahunala, exemplifies such a concern of a migrant. Tadvis are at the top of the social order in Mahunala.

Before Navalsingh took up trading, like most youths in Mahunala, he was migrating seasonally. Navalsingh had studied up to tenth standard. His father sent him out for studies. Navalsingh married a woman who was educated up to eighth standard. Navalsingh's family is quite big. They are five sons and three daughters to their parents. Despite having over five acres of land, the compulsion for migration was always there to meet the family's additional needs. Navalsingh's father also used to go for seasonal migration. But a burn injury suffered while working on a road construction made him not to go for migration thereafter. Navalsingh, along with his wife and brothers, was migrating to Ahmedabad for construction work. He became a mason and was able to earn good income with his wife. Both were able to save considerable amount. However, Navalsingh was slowly getting dejected of leading a migrant's life, particularly living with wife and children in open and unprotected places in cities. He wanted to come back to the village and start some activity on his own. The death of his ten-year old nephew in a road accident during migration was the last straw. Soon after, he stopped migration and started a small grocery shop out of own savings and a bank loan. Navalsingh's wife had earlier undergone a training in tailoring. They also started a tailoring business only to give up later on as the demand for service was dwindling.

Navalsingh now has a pretty good trading business in the village. Besides running a grocery shop, he also does foodgrains trading. Recently, he got a loan sanctioned under a self-employment scheme to expand his foodgrains business. He also obtained a training in poultry farming and is keen to start a small farm to sell eggs.

Navalsingh got separated from his parents six years ago. The family land is still undivided. His parents live with other children. Navalsingh would like to help his brothers to take up self-employment like him. His brothers still migrate seasonally for construction work. Navalsingh is building a new pucca house costing Rs. 30,000 in the village. He proudly says that he contributes annually about Rs. 25,000 towards *chandlavidhi.* He is very keen to educate all his children.

Having successfully transformed himself from a migrant to an entrepreneur, Navalsingh is quite indignant of fellow villagers who migrate in hordes. To him, "their status is like a broken pot which can never be put together again or like a dog's tail which cannot be mended".

At the village level itself, though a government wage employment programme is being implemented, it cannot also arrest the large scale migration because of its inability to offer reliable and significant level of employment under various public works.

It is because of the above reasons, majority of the households in Mahudi and Mahunala look towards seasonal, casual and unskilled but reliable employment available in far off rural and urban areas.

5. CONCLUSION

To sum up, for a majority of the tribal households in Mahudi and Mahunala faced with the constraint of declining local resource base to support their livelihood and lack of any suitable local alternatives, distress seasonal migration to places of assured employment seems to have become a major support for livelihood survival. Unlike in the past, the avenues of livelihood for these households are split between their own meagre agricultural base and distance seasonal migration. These findings are clearly supportive of the first part of the major hypothesis raised by us that the livelihood systems in semi-arid areas are increasingly becoming dependent on external sources to varied consequences. Apart from the economic compulsion of ensuring food security, quite a few factors including some of the social practices of the Bhils are found to be playing a significant role in determining the magnitude of diversification. Thus, diversification also gets determined by an interplay of socio-economic factors. While diversification by way of seasonal migration seems to have ensured the livelihood survival for many households and some level of consolidation for a few households; drawing of any firm inferences on the overall issue of livelihood sustainability, however, would require examining certain other dimensions of diversification like the consequences of increased external dependence. Having seen the extent and nature of diversification in the villages dominated by the tribal households, in the next chapter we examine the nature of occupational diversification in Bodiya, a caste based village having relatively better socio-economic endowments.

4

OCCUPATIONAL DIVERSIFICATION IN A CASTE-BASED VILLAGE

1. INTRODUCTION

The present chapter deals with the phenomenon of occupational diversification in a caste-based village, viz. Bodiya situated in the semi-arid Saurashtra region of Gujarat. Compared to the tribal villages like Mahudi and Mahunala, caste-based villages exhibit wide differentiation in the socio-economic status and endowments across different sections living in the village. Such a differentiation is likely to have a significant impact on the livelihood strategies adopted by households belonging to different sections. It was with the purpose of capturing the impact of socio-economic differentiation on the process of occupational diversification, the village Bodiya was selected for the present study. Bodiya was one of the three villages selected for the larger research study (see Chapter One) based on a criterion identified to suit the requirements of the larger study. The analysis in the Chapter is based on the data drawn mainly from a sample survey of 66 households representing various sections in the village. Besides, the analysis in the Chapter is also supplemented by a few household case studies and group discussions carried out during the study.

The Chapter is divided into five sections including the introduction. In Section 2, the profile of Bodiya in terms of its resource base and socio-economic characteristics of the households is presented. Section 3 deals with the nature of occupational diversification in Bodiya. The impact of diversification on the livelihood of different sections is presented in Section 4. Section 5 draws a brief conclusion about the nature of occupational diversification observed in Bodiya.

2. PROFILE OF BODIYA

2.1. Location and Resources

Bodiya is situated in Limbdi taluka of Surendranagar district. The village is about 9 kms from Limbdi town, the taluka headquarters. The village lies on the national highway that connects Rajkot and Ahmedabad. Bodiya has a history that is more than 300 years old, according to the village elders. The village occupied a prominent place under the dynasty of Rajputs that ruled the Limbdi province. According to the village elders, the name of the village earlier was Ghadvada and was later named as Bodiya due to the Swayambhu Bodeshwar Mahadev temple built about 300 years back.

The economic and social links between Bodiya and other towns are well established. The village is well connected to Limbdi, a cotton trading and diamond-polishing centre, and Chuda, known for cumin trade. In addition to these connections based on trade and employment, caste and kinship relations also provide the basis of extensive social links with other villages and towns.

The village falls in the semi-arid tracts of Western India. The climate is characterised by hot summers and general dryness except during the South-West monsoon season (June to September). The average annual rainfall in the region is about 506.88 mm, and about 94 per cent of the annual rainfall is received from the South-West monsoon. Bhogavo river flows through the village from west to east and lies on south of the village. The river remains dry for most of the year. The river derives its peculiar name from the regular pattern of rapid flowing out, as the terrain is a bit sloppy. During the monsoon months the river swells up and is reasonably turbulent, but soon afterwards the water disappears.

The lands are gently undulating with highlands in the western and southern part of the village. The soils are of sandy-loamy type with a coarse structure and in some parts there is a good amount of clay present. This kind of structure helps in providing a good water retaining capacity, which is suitable for the cultivation of cotton, the major cash crop grown in the district and in the village.

The total geographical area of the village is 2068.07 acres and its distribution by different uses is shown in Table 4.1. The residential area of the village is 10.19 acres and all the houses are clustered into it. Over the years, the residential area has been slowly expanding. The cultivable land which is the most important resource base of the village accounts for about 70.4 per cent of the total area. However, as described elsewhere the cultivable land is distributed highly unequally across different sections of the village. Nearly 12 per cent of the total area is under wastelands. Part of the wastelands has been distributed by government to the landless for cultivation. *Gauchar* land, meant for grazing purpose, accounts for about 4.4 per cent of the total area.

Table 4.1
Geographical Area of Bodiya Village

(Area in acres)

	Area	*(in %)*
Cultivable Land	1455.37	70.4
Waste Lands	241.89	11.7
River Canal Lands	218.30	10.6
Common Lands	6.92	0.33
Residential Area *Gauchar* Ponds Highway Common Threshing Land	10.19 90.02 1.30 34.33 3.21	0.49 4.35 0.06 1.66 0.16
Boundary Bunds	0.11	0.01
Non Agricultural Lands	10.06	0.49
Total Land	2068.07	100.0

Source: Bodiya Village Panchayat Records, 1997.

Demography : The total population of Bodiya village as per the 1991 Census was 945, consisting of 165 households. The sex ratio in the village was 882 females per 1000 men. As per the estimation based on the sample survey carried out in 1997, the population in Bodiya was 1154 with an average household size of 5.95. The density of population is about 138 persons per square kilometre. Interestingly, the enumeration of households through PRA method revealed existence of 232 households in the village. However, the actual number of households in the village was only 194, the rest 38 households belonging mostly to Patel (traditionally known as Patidars) and Bharwaad castes have over the years migrated permanently from the village in search of various occupations. Most of these permanent migrant households own land and house in the village. The members of these households visit the village during festivals and other social occasions. Their kins still consider them as residents of the village. Those who own land have entrusted the responsibility of land management either to their relatives or to other villagers on lease or share cropping basis.

The literacy rate in the village was about 46 per cent as per the 1991 census, with the male and the female literacy rates being 55 per cent and 32 per cent respectively. There is a middle school established about 50 years back in the village. The level of literacy of the sample population (1997) was 64 per cent. The male literacy rate was 74.9 per cent and the female literacy rate was 49.7 per cent.

2.2 Caste and Social Structure in Bodiya

The village is composed of households belonging to several castes (Table 4.2). There are in all fourteen castes, which include a majority of peasants and a few priestly, service, artisan and the untouchable castes. All the caste groups are located along different streets. The plan of the village reflects the caste hierarchy with the Patels (Patidars) and the Darbaars at the centre of the village and the other castes along the different corners. The Pagi, Bhangi and Vaaghri households reside on the outskirts of the village, and quite a few of them also live on farms alienated from the village. The Pagi, Bhangi, Vaaghri and Chamar are the untouchable castes and these households mostly live in mud houses.

Table 4.2

Caste-wise Distribution of Households in Bodiya

Caste	*Number of Households (HHs)*	*Number of HHs Surveyed*	*Permanent Migrant HHs.*
Patel	62	14	27
Darbaar	41	12	-
Maharaj/Gosain	7	2	-
Koli Patel	29	9	-
Dalwaadi	15	5	-
Bharwaad	31	6	10
Kumbhaar	11	5	1
Valand	2	2	-
Lohaar	2	1	-
Raawal	1	-	-
Pagi	11	3	-
Bhangi	4	3	-
Vaaghri	13	4	-
Chamar	3	-	-
Total	232	66	38

Source: As per enumeration made in Bodiya, 1997

The caste status in the village corresponds closely with the economic activity pursued. But over the period, a number of castes have diversified from their traditional activity and are engaged in various other non-farm activities. A brief analysis of various castes in the village and their socio-economic status is given below.

The Patels who comprise 26.7 per cent of the households in the village are both the most numerous of the castes and also the owners of the major part of the land (32.5 per cent) in the village. They are thus dominant both in terms of their number and control over land. The Patels are the cultivating caste whose main occupation is agriculture. But over the years, the Patels have diversified into a number of other non-farm activities.

The Darbaars who comprise 17.7 per cent of the households and control about one-fourth of the land are independent of any domination as a group from the Patels. Though the Patels and the Darbaars are the dominant castes in the village, there exist some differences between these two castes in their social organisation. One of the differences is the *'Purdah'* system followed by Darbaars wherein the women are not allowed outside the four walls and they are not supposed to speak to other men. The housing structure of the Darbaars clearly depicts the system they follow as the houses have huge doors for enclosing. The female labour force participation among the Darbaars is very low. The Darbaar's main occupation is agriculture and they have also diversified into many non-farm activities like diamond polishing.

Apart from Patels and Darbaars, the other upper castes in the village are Maharaj and Gosains who constitute 3 per cent of the households. The Maharaj and Gosains are priests of the village. They perform rituals during festivals and also maintain the temples including the temple lands.

After Patel and Darbaars, Koli Patels and Dalwadis are the next important landed castes in the village. The Koli Patels who comprise about 12.5 per cent of the households own about 15 per cent of the land. Besides agriculture, the Koli Patels also pursue other non-farm occupations like trading and diamond polishing. The Dalwaadis are the traditional vegetable growers but there seems to be no trace of this occupation today. The Dalwaadis have diversified into other cash crop cultivation, diamond polishing, embroidery and other activities.

The Bharwaads who comprise about 13 per cent of households are the herdsmen or the cattle grazing community of the village. The Bharwaads own cows, sheep and goats, though over the years their cattle population has been on a decline. The responsibility for grazing the cattle of the village rests with Bharwaads. Some of them also own land. Each Bharwaad household takes care of the cattle of the village for a year on a rotational basis. They are paid in kind for their customary services.

The Kumbhaars are the traditional potters of the village. Pottery has declined tremendously over the years and agriculture has become the predominant occupation for these families. Some of the Kumbhaars have also diversified into non-farm activities like trading and diamond polishing. There are only three households in the village who continue with pottery even now. The decline in pottery has been mainly due to the replacement of mud vessels by metal utensils, and modern tiles have replaced traditional tiles. Each Kumbhaar family serves a group of households in the village. There are about forty households under each Kumbhaar family. The Kumbhaar households get paid for their service. People from neighbouring villages also buy pots and other mud vessels from them.

There are two barber households who belong to Valand caste and reside in the village. The entire village is divided between these two barbers and they receive payment mostly in kind for their customary services. Every household pays them 10 kgs of foodgrain every year or Rs. 60 in cash in case they are landless. They are also called upon to provide band services during village weddings and festivals. There are two Lohaar households engaged in blacksmithy and carpentry work. The village is also composed of three Chamaars and one Raawal households who live outside the village. The Chamaars who are the cobblers reside in a nearby village even though they possess land in Bodiya. According to some people, the Chamaars who are untouchables are forced to live outside the village because of a curse.

The Bhangi (4), Pagi (11) and Vaaghri (13) castes are the other untouchable castes in the village. These households form the class of agricultural labourers in the village. Some of them own land received under a land distribution scheme in the village. Though constituting about 13.5 per cent of the total households, the untouchable castes own only about 3 per cent of the land. The Vaaghris have their own small hamlet in one of the corners of the village. They work as agricultural labourers for the higher castes. Except the Bhangis, none of the lower caste households are found performing any traditional occupation. The Bhangis also perform as drummers in the village during festivals and funerals. The untouchables are at the bottom of the social ladder in the village. Despite some of them pursuing new occupations, their social status remains the same.

2.3 Land and Water

To understand what kind of production relations exists, it may become essential to look at resource asymmetry and caste hierarchy. As could be made out from the above section, not only there is differentiation in terms of caste status across different households but also in terms of ownership of land. As per the sample survey, about one-fourth of the households are landless. Most of these landless households are from middle and lower castes like Koli Patel, Bharwaads, Kumbhaar, Bhangi, Pagi and Vaaghri. Even among the landed households, constituting about 74 per cent of the total, land ownership is inequitably distributed. Though the average land owned by landed households is 9.31 acres, across different caste groups the variation is from 0.65 acres in the case of Pagis to about 22 acres in the case of Darbaars. (Table 4.3) The land distribution in the village is skewed in favour of the upper castes.

Table 4.3
Caste-wise Landholding Distribution

Caste	*Number of Households*	*Land Owned (in acres)*	*Proportion (%) to total land holding*	*Land Owned per Household (in acre)*
Patel	14 (1)	148.28	32.49	11.41
Darbaar	12 (1)	115.66	25.34	22.18
Maharaj/ Gosain	2	12.00	2.63	6.00
Koli Patel	9 (3)	70.16	15.37	11.69
Dalwaadi	5	65.62	14.38	13.12
Bharwaad	6 (4)	11.50	2.52	5.75
Kumbhaar	5 (2)	14.08	3.09	4.69
Valand	2 (1)	5.00	1.10	5.00
Lohaar	1 (1)	0.00	0.00	0.00
Pagi	3 (1)	1.30	0.29	0.65
Bhangi	3 (2)	5.00	1.10	5.00
Vaaghri	4 (1)	7.80	1.71	2.60
Total	66 (17)	456.40	100.0	9.31

Source: Sample Survey of 66 Households in Bodiya Village, 1997.
Note: Figures in brackets are the number of landless households.

Many of the lower caste households who own land have been the beneficiaries of land distribution by the government. As per the Panchayat sources, there has been distribution of government land in the village on six occasions during 1959 to 1982. The land was distributed to about 12 households belonging to Koli Patel, Bharwaad, Pagi, Vaaghri, Chamaar, Bhangi and Raawal castes. A total of 44.97 acres of land has been distributed to these households.

The land lease market in the village is active with a number of lease transactions taking place annually. However, leasing-in land by the landless is almost absent in the village. Those who lease-in lands are mostly from the Patel and Darbaar castes. Land leasing seems to be helping the land owning households to further consolidate their landholding position.

Groundwater is the major source for meeting domestic and agricultural water needs. If we look at the development of well irrigation in the village, we find that the wells have been constructed as far back as 1930s. Farmers were used to several traditional ways of water lifting. The introduction of oil engine in the 1950s enabled the farmers to invest money to lift more water. A number of wells came to be dug on the village riverbed.

There are about 66 wells in the village for irrigation, out of which 34 of them are on the riverbed. The normal depth of a working well is about 40 feet. The wells on the riverbed have been connected to fields by underground pipelines of 500 to 3,300 feet distance. If we look at the ownership pattern of the wells in the village, we find that out of the 66 wells, 33 wells are owned by the Patels, 21 of them by the Darbaars, seven by the Koli Patels, two by the Dalwaadis and one each by Kumbhaar, Bharwaad and Pagi households. The ownership pattern of wells thus is not only unequal across caste groups but as a result has widened the inequality arising out of land distribution.

However, the wells are mostly owned and used on a shared basis. If we look at the wells of the sample households surveyed, we find that the 32 wells are shared by 69 families. Again, out of the 32 wells, 14 wells are under individual ownership and 18 wells are under joint ownership.

The water market in the village is quite active during both kharif and rabi seasons. As the Patels and the Darbaars own most of the wells, they comprise the major sellers of the water in the market. This places them in a position of advantage to consolidate their economic base further.

3. OCCUPATIONAL DIVERSIFICATION IN BODIYA

The present section has two parts. The first part deals with the overall structure of occupational diversification prevailing in Bodiya. The objective is to get an idea about the extent and magnitude of different occupations pursued in Bodiya. The second part tries to analyse the nature and extent of diversification that has taken place across different socio-economic categories in the village.

3.1 Occupational Structure

As could be made out from the analysis in Section 2, there is a close relationship between caste, ownership of resources and the primary occupations pursued by the households belonging to different sections in Bodiya. However, one can at the same time observe some influence of the forces of development and modernisation on the prevailing occupational structure. Agriculture remains the main occupation pursued by a majority of the households. As per the sample survey, about 70 per cent of the households are pursuing agriculture (Table 4.4). Since landholding in the

Table 4.4
Occupational Structure in Bodiya, 1997

Occupations	*No. of Households*	*Proportion to total (%)*
(1)	(2)	(3)
Agriculture	46	69.7
Agriculture labour	21 (1)	31.8
Animal husbandry	8 (1)	12.1
Artisanry	14 (1)	21.2
Services	19 (7)	28.7
Trade and Business	8 (1)	12.1
Diamond Polishing	36 (18)	54.6

Source: Sample survey of 66 households.
NB: Because of the multiple occupations pursued by the households there is an overlap in the number of households in column (2). Figures in parentheses are the number of households whose members migrate for work.

village is inequally distributed across different sections, the extent of livelihood support derived from agriculture in terms of food, income and employment also varies significantly across the households. A significant proportion of the households (about 32 per cent) also depend on agriculture indirectly by pursuing agricultural labour work. Though it is mainly the landless households from the lower castes who undertake agricultural labour work, households owning small landholdings belonging to middle and upper castes also take up agricultural labour work. Thus, an overwhelming proportion of the households depend upon agriculture, directly or indirectly for their livelihood.

Animal husbandry is the primary source of livelihood for about 12 per cent of the households. Though many households keep animals, animal husbandry is a major occupation among the Bharwaads. Besides agriculture and animal husbandry, one can observe that a number of other occupations also exist in the village. While some of the existing non-farm occupations are traditional, many new or modern occupations also have emerged recently in the village. Broadly, four categories of non-farm occupations may be noticed, viz., artisans, services, trade and business and diamond polishing. These non-farm activities are pursued both by the landed and landless households but with variation in the type of activity pursued and the extent of involvement. About 21 per cent of the households are involved in various artisanal activities like pottery, blacksmith, carpentry, spinning and embroidery. Spinning and embroidery has come to the village fairly recently. Spinning as an income earning activity is pursued mostly by the women of the Darbaar caste for whom there are restrictions to participate in activities carried outside the household. Spinning with the help of motorised *charkha* (wheel) has proved to be quite handy for these women to supplement their family income during the lean periods. Similarly, a few young women of the Dalwaadi caste are pursuing embroidery as a supplementary activity.

Service is another category of non-farm occupations in which a significant proportion (29 per cent) of the households are engaged in. Even under this category, one can observe the prevalence of both traditional and modern types of occupations. Priests, drum beaters and barbers are some of the traditional service providers found in Bodiya. However, the bulk of the activities under this category are of modern types which include public works contract, motor driving, tractor service and government or quasi-government jobs like teachers, clerks, sweepers, cleaners and attendants. The traditional service occupations are pursued by households belonging to castes like Maharaj, Valand and Bhangi; the modern ones are pursued by households belonging to all castes. Trade and business is the third category of non-farm occupations. About 12 per cent of the sample households were found engaged in activities like foodgrains trade, condiments shop, flour mill, tailoring and typewriting training. The trade and business activities are carried out mostly by households belonging to the upper and middle castes like Patel, Darbaar and Kumbhaar.

The most significant non-farm occupation which has emerged recently in Bodiya is diamond polishing. A large number of households, accounting for nearly 55 per cent of the total which is next only to agriculture, are now pursuing diamond polishing. Though the diamond polishing activity in the village has started in the 1980s, people from Bodiya have been migrating to Surat since early 1970s for diamond polishing work. A significant number of households, particularly belonging to the Patel caste, have migrated permanently to Surat and Ahmedabad in search of diamond polishing work. A few are also the owners of diamond polishing units set up in the village. Members of most of the households work as skilled labourers in the diamond polishing units both within and outside the village.

An important aspect of the occupational diversification in Bodiya, as may be seen from Table 4.4, is that members from a considerable number of households migrate out daily or seasonally to nearby and far-off places for pursuing various non-farm occupations. About 38 per cent of the sample households are resorting to such migration. Migration can be seen (Table 4.4) mostly in the case of households pursuing service and diamond polishing, the latter accounting for 72 per cent of the migrating households. Except for agriculture, households migrate under all other categories of occupations, though in varying numbers.

3.2 Occupational Diversification by Socio-Economic Category

The occupational structure of Bodiya is thus a diversified one though agriculture continues to dominate as a source of livelihood for most of the households. As could be seen, there is considerable variation in the social status and resources endowments of households belonging to different sections in Bodiya. When there is occupational diversification under such a situation, which are the different sections that stand to gain from the process? In order to find an answer to the above question, an attempt is made in this part to examine the extent of diversification that has taken place across different socio-economic categories. The analysis is done mainly by identifying the proportion or number of households who have diversified across different socio-economic categories in Bodiya. A diversified household is defined here as one which has taken up any new source of income or employment to supplement its traditional or main occupation. In order to identify the socio-economic categories, all the sample households have been classified both based on the status of their caste and the extent of land ownership. In terms of caste status, the households are categorized into three broad groups viz, lower, middle and upper caste groups. The categorization is based mainly on the understanding gained by us about the overall status of different castes in the village during the study. All the untouchable castes viz., Pagi, Bhangi, and Vaaghri are categorised under lower caste group. The Patel, Darbaar and Maharaj/Gosain castes which are at top of the village social hierarchy are categorized under the upper caste group. The rest are classified under the middle caste group.

In terms of economic status, the sample households have been categorized into six groups based on the extent of land owned by them. Extent of land owned is considered here as a proxy for the economic status of a household; higher the land owned higher is the economic status. The six land size groups are: landless, 0 to 2.5 acres, 2.5 to 5 acres, 5 to 10 acres, 10 to 20 acres, and 20 acres and above.

Tables 4.5 and 4.6 present data on the extent of diversification by caste status and land-size groups. It may be seen that about 77 per cent of the sample households in Bodiya have diversified from their traditional or main occupation by taking up some new source of income and employment. Thus, bulk of the households has adopted diversification.

Table 4.5
Occupational Diversification by Caste Status in Bodiya

Caste Status	*Number of Sample House-holds*	*Proportion of Diversi-fied House-holds (%)*	*Activities of Diversified Households(%)*			
			Diamond Polishing	*Services*	*Artisanry*	*Trade and Business*
(1)	(2)	(3)	(4)	(5)	(6)	(7)
Lower	10	50.0 (5)	40.0 (2)	60.0 (3)	-	-
Middle	28	71.4 (20)	75.0 (15)	20.0 (4)	5.0 (1)	30.0(6)
Upper	28	92.9 (26)	73.1 (19)	34.6 (9)	15.4 (4)	7.7 (2)
Total	66	77.3 (51)	70.6 (36)	31.4 (16)	9.8 (5)	15.7 (8)

Source: Sample survey of 66 households. Figures in parentheses are actual number of households.

Note: Because more than one diversified occupations pursued by many households, the percentages in columns 4 to 7 may not add up to hundred.

However, the extent of diversification varies across different socio-economic categories. Across different castes (Table 4.5), the proportion of diversified households increases clearly with the increase in the caste status. Higher the caste status, higher is the extent of diversification. The proportion of diversified households increases from 50 per cent in the case of lower castes to 71.4 per cent in the case of middle castes to 93 per cent in the case of upper castes. If we look at the extent of diversification by land-size groups, though bulk of households under all groups have diversified but the proportion of diversified households is much higher in the case of bigger land-size groups as compared to smaller land-size groups (Table 4.6). Interestingly, the landless group which consists of households from all castes shows a much higher level of diversification than the small and marginal

Table 4.6
Occupational Diversification by Land Ownership in Bodiya

Land-Size Group (in acres)	*Number of Sample House-holds*	*Proportion of Diversi-fied House-holds (%)*	*Activities of Diversified Households(%)*			
			Diamond Polishing	*Services*	*Artisanry*	*Trade and Business*
(1)	*(2)*	*(3)*	*(4)*	*(5)*	*(6)*	*(7)*
Landless	17	76.5 (13)	53.90 (7)	23.1 (3)	15.4 (2)	30.8 (4)
0-2.5	9	66.7 (6)	66.7 (4)	33.3 (2)	-	16.7 (1)
2.5-5	13	69.2 (9)	77.8 (7)	11.1 (1)	-	22.2 (2)
5-10	13	84.6 (11)	81.8 (9)	27.3 (3)	18.2 (2)	-
10-20	9	88.9 (8)	62.5 (5)	50.0 (4)	-	-
> 20	5	80.0 (4)	100.0 (4)	75.0 (3)	25.0 (1)	25.0 (1)
Total	66	77.3 (51)	70.6 (36)	31.4 (16)	9.8. (5)	15.7 (8)

Source: Sample survey of 66 households. Figures in parentheses are actual number of households.

Note: Because of more than one diversified occupations pursued by many households, the percentages in columns 4 to 7 do not add up to hundred.

land-size groups. This could be attributed partly to the relative compulsion of landless households to diversify for supplementing their livelihood from the main or traditional occupation as compared to the land owning households. Overall, though a major portion of the households in Bodiya have got diversified there is a clear variation in the extent of diversification across different sections. The extent of diversification is higher for the household groups which are in the upper socio-economic strata.

From Table 4.5 and 4.6 one can also see data on the extent of diversification into various types of occupations by households in different socio-economic groups. It may be seen that households in Bodiya have diversified into four types of occupations viz., diamond polishing, services, artisanry and trade and business. The different activities pursued under services, artisanry and trade and business are same as those mentioned in Section 2 of the present Chapter. Diamond polishing is the major type of diversified activity. About 71 per cent of the diversified households are pursuing diamond polishing. Though households belonging to all sections pursue diamond polishing but the proportion is higher for households in the upper strata of both castes and land-size categories. Services consisting of various types of private or governmental jobs are the second major category. About 31.4 per cent of the diversified households are into various types of service activities. Under services, one can not see any clear pattern across different caste and land-size groups. Unlike diamond polishing, the service activities pursued are of various types. Hence different households have been able to take up different service activities depending upon their capabilities. In fact for the lower caste households (Table 4.5), service activities appear to be a major type of diversification. These are mainly petty government jobs which they have been able to obtain due to job reservation policy of the State. Similarly, services are also an important category of diversification for the top two land-size groups. Regarding trade and business, and artisanry, if we look at from the caste angle, it is only the households in the middle and upper caste groups who have taken up these activities. However, in terms of land-size groups there is no clear pattern though it is mostly the landless who have diversified into trade and business. For the landless, trade and business is the second important category of diversification after diamond polishing.

To sum up, the analysis of occupational diversification by socio-economic status reveals that the extent of overall diversification by different household groups shows a clear relationship with the status of the group. Higher the status of the group, higher is the extent of diversification by households under the group. Diamond polishing which is the major form of diversification also shows a similar relationship when seen from both the land ownership and caste status. In terms of other occupations, there are variations in the relationship as the activities pursued are of diverse types requiring varied skills and capabilities.

4. IMPACT OF DIVERSIFICATION ON LIVELIHOOD IN BODIYA

Bodiya, thus, exhibits occupational diversification of a significant order. All sections of the households in the village have diversified though in varying degree determined mainly by their socio-economic status. As a result of the variation in the nature and extent of diversification across different sections, the impact of the process on the livelihood also has been of a varying nature.

In the present section an attempt is made to assess the nature of the impact of occupational diversification in Bodiya. The first part presents the utilization pattern of the earnings from the diversified activities of the sample households. In the second part, the impact is captured through case study of three households representing three different socio-economic categories in Bodiya. The third part tries to capture the impact of broader economic changes taking place in Bodiya including occupation diversification on the livelihood status of different sections.

4.1 Utilisation Pattern of Earnings by Diversified Households

How far the diversification process has been helpful in the sustainability of livelihood for the households can be made out from the pattern of utilization of earnings from the diversified sources of income. An attempt was made during the household survey in Bodiya to find out the major purposes for which the earnings are being utilized. Table 4.7 presents a broad picture of the utilization pattern for 51 diversified households. It must be mentioned here that most households spend the income on multiple purposes. The households also have multiple sources of income. Hence, data on the exact magnitude of spending on different purposes could not be collected.

Table 4.7

Utilisation Pattern of Earnings from Diversified Activities in Bodiya

Purposes	*Number of Households*
1. Household purposes	50
2. Agricultural Production	19
3. Trade and Business	6
4. House Construction/ Renovation	14
5. Assets	7
6. Local Loan Repayment	21

Source: Survey of 51 households who have diversified their occupations in Bodiya.

Note: Most households use the earnings for multiple purposes.

Going by Table 4.7, one can make out that almost all the households (50 of 51) are utilizing the earnings from their diversified sources for meeting various household needs like food, clothing, education and health. Diversification, thus, appears to have become an important source of income for supplementing the livelihood from agriculture and other traditional occupations. In the case of households whose members have migrated to other places because of diversification, earnings from the diversified activity is the key source for the maintenance of family in the migrant place. Such a pattern is seen especially in the case of households who have migrated for diamond polishing work.

While meeting household needs is the dominant purpose, many households utilize their earnings for production purposes also. About 37 per cent of the households reported utilizing the earnings for buying inputs and labour for agricultural production. Given the fact that the cost of agricultural production has gone up because of intensification, additional earnings from the diversified activity for these households has become a useful source of meeting the enhanced cost. Similarly, some households (6) have diverted their earnings for investing in trade and business. Partly, diversification is thus facilitating production or income generating activity aimed at ensuring livelihood security.

Interestingly, about 41 per cent of the households reported utilizing the income from diversified source for repayment of loan taken for meeting both production and household needs. As per the sample survey, about 64 per cent of the households borrow from formal or informal sources in Bodiya; the major purpose of borrowing being meeting of household needs. For the households who have diversified, the earnings from the new occupation seem to be playing a crucial role in enhancing both their borrowing and repayment capacity.

For some, the earnings are also a source for consolidating their livelihood status and security. This is evident from the fact that the earnings in the case of many households are finding their way out for investing in house construction or renovation and purchase of productive or household assets. About 14 of the 51 households reported that part of cost of house construction carried out either in the village or at the migrant place, was met from the earnings of the diversified activity. Members of many of the households who have migrated for diamond polishing work in cities like Ahmedabad and Surat have built their own houses. Regular income from diamond polishing has helped them in making such an investment. Again a few households (7) have invested part of their earnings for acquiring assets like well, tractor, and motor vehicle. For these households diversification has become an avenue for strengthening their livelihood base. However, an examination of the socio-economic characteristic of the households showed that the households who are able to utilize the earnings for such purposes are mainly from the well-off categories. In other words, while diversification is supplementing the livelihood sustenance of all sections, for the relatively well-off, it has also become a means for consolidating their economic base.

4.2 Three Faces of Diversification in Bodiya

In order to gain more qualitative insights into the nature and impact of the process of diversification in Bodiya, we carried out case studies of three households who belong to different socio-economic categories. Described below are three such household case studies capturing three different facets of the impact.

Hard Way to Survival : The Case of Meghji and Savriben

Meghji Meru Sitapara is a landless labourer aged about 52 years. These days, for Meghji and his wife Savri, aged 50 years, the lean period survival strategy is one of making charcoal from the thorny bush of Ganda Baval. It was for the first time they are making charcoal on their own for sale.

Meghji and Savri belong to the untouchable Pagi caste. Meghji claims he is able to read and write as he did some schooling, though the rest of his family members including his son Eshwar (22 years old) are illiterate.

Meghji has encroached a small piece of village pasture land on which he does some agriculture. Being poor, there has not been any objection by the other villagers to Meghji's encroachment. Meghji and Savri are making charcoal on this land by collecting the wood of Ganda Baval from the nearby wastelands. Meghji claims because of his acquaintance with the local government officials, he faces no problem in collecting the wood for the purpose. Meghji has learnt coal making by working as a labourer for the contractors who had come from Kutch to the area for making charcoal. Labouring together Meghji and Savri are able to make about 400-500 kgs of coal per week. The activity is carried out for 2-3 months during summer. The coal is sold to nearby hotels located on the highway at the rate of Rs. 2.50 per kg.

Not totally happy with charcoal making, Meghji believes that it is in his fate that he has to pursue such an occupation.

Primarily, Meghji, his wife and daughter-in-law work as farm labourers for the Patel and Darbaar households. The work is available mainly during the agricultural season spread over four months. Weeding, pruning and harvesting of cotton, bajra and sesame are the major farm works performed. Though the wage rate varies across operations, a person day of labour fetches them Rs. 30 along with some vegetables, buttermilk and tea. Other types of work done include cotton depodding and plant uprooting. Since the agricultural labour work is only seasonal, Meghji has to look for other avenues during rest of the year for sustenance. Meghji also carries out carpentry work whenever available, both within and outside the village. In case of dire need, he borrows money from the households for whom he works as a labourer. The loan is normally repaid by rendering farm work.

Meghji's son, Eshwar, who failed to go to school, has taken up diamond polishing work in the village. Working for the last five years, he earns about Rs. 1,200 per month, just enough to ensure sustenance for him and his wife.

Being landless and illiterate, under the present circumstances Meghji's family has only a very limited opportunity for attaining any real advancement in the livelihood despite the diversification.

Advancement through Diversification: The Case of Prabhu Mohan's Family

For a household having already a well secured livelihood, opening up of any new avenue earning can only help in its further consolidation. This is the experience of Prabhu Mohan Patel owning about 40 acres of land and his children are diversified into diamond polishing for the last 12 years. Three of the four sons of Prabhu Mohan are settled in Ahmedabad working in diamond polishing units.

Being a landed family, the initial impetus for consolidation has come from developments in agriculture. Prabhu Mohan bought a riverbed well from a local farmer about 30 years ago. By making his own investment, Prabhu Mohan laid about 300 feet of pipeline for irrigating the land. Though the well irrigates only about 5 acres of land but it was of immense help in ensuring family's livelihood security in the context of recurring droughts. At the same time, Prabhu Mohan could also go in for commercial and modern agriculture. Cotton and sesame became the major crops grown. There was adoption of improved varieties of crops and use of chemical fertilizers for yield enhancement. The family's landholding expanded with Prabhu Mohan buying 5 acres of land from a local villager during a drought year.

The family's better-off economic conditions helped all the children to get some education though only till primary or middle school. Realising that agriculture cannot support all the members, the household decided to diversify. Employment in the growing diamond polishing work became the obvious choice of diversification for the sons. It was Mahadev, the eldest son, who first went to Surat. But unable to pick up the skill fully, Mahadev returned to Bodiya and decided to help his father in the agricultural work. The other three sons being deft joined diamond polishing on a regular basis. For the family, diversification of the sons into diamond polishing became a major way of supplementing the agricultural livelihood. For the sons, as described by their mother, it was a way out from the drudgery of agricultural work.

Having picked up the necessary skill and understanding about diamond polishing, the three sons even started unsuccessfully their own diamond polishing unit in partnership with an outsider. The failure of the venture, made them to work for other units in Ahmedabad. The three brothers specialize mainly in diamond cleaning and cutting and earn about Rs. 8000 to 10,000 per month each. These three sons now live separately with their families in Ahmedabad. Having established themselves in diamond polishing, two of the three brothers have built their own houses. They also got a support of Rs. 25,000 each from their family in the village for house construction. The third son resides in a rented house. All the three send part of their income back home annually. At the same time they get foodgrains from the family produce.

In the village, it is Mahadev who looks after agriculture in the absence of other three brothers. Mahadev being able to pursue agriculture on a full time basis, there is enough attention being given to land. During 1996-97, they bought 20 trucks of farmyard manure from outside at a cost of Rs. 30,000. Because of the increased farm work, they have disposed of their bullocks and have bought a tractor by investing about Rs. 3.3 lakh. While part of the investment (Rs. 2 lakh) for the tractor was borrowed from their relatives, the rest came from own sources including remittances from the city. The tractor in turn has become an additional source of income with Mahadev able to earn about Rs. 15,000 per annum by hiring out its services to other households in the village.

The diversification by three sons has helped the family primarily by reducing the pressure on agriculture. Agriculture has been further strengthened by investments supported by remittances. A new urban link has been established in the process. Now, all the five children of Mahadev are in Ahmedabad residing with their uncles and pursuing their schooling. The three sons visit the family during festivals and are considered as an integral part of the family and village life. Their names continue to appear on the village voters' list.

A person who respects family traditions and appreciates the value of education, especially for girls, Prabhu Mohan intends to partition the land among his sons after marrying off his last daughter Nita. He has a plan to build soon a new house for the family in the village, a sign of improved prosperity.

Push towards Nomadism: The Case of Manji Moti Bharwaad

The Bharwaads are the traditional cowherds in the village. Besides rearing own cattle, they also help in grazing the cattle of other households in the village for which they get paid in cash and kind. They make their livelihood by selling milk, milk products and manure. Agriculture supplements the livelihood of those who own some land. Not all the Bharwaad households own land, and those who own, possess only very small holdings. Being livestock based, the security of livelihood for the Bharwaads depends greatly on the adequate availability of water and fodder. A reliable market for their livestock products is also an important factor determining their well-being. Over the years, in Bodiya the Bharwaads have been experiencing deterioration in the availability of fodder and water as well as difficulty in marketing of milk and milk products remuneratively. The increase in the cropping intensity and a decline in the availability of grazing land because of expansion of agricultural land has severely affected maintenance of their livestock. Besides, the difficulty in marketing of milk either because of lack of adequate local demand or absence of organized effort has forced Bharwaads to adopt varied coping strategies for survival. While some have reduced drastically the strength of their livestock and have tried to diversify into other occupations, others have resorted to migration even to far-off places in search of greener pastures both for themselves and their livestock.

The experience of Manji Moti is illustrative of the plight of Bharwaads who have been compelled to lead almost a nomadic life. Manji Moti a landless and an illiterate Bharwaad had about 100 cows. Manji Moti's family migrated to Amaravati in Maharashtra a decade back with all their livestock. Some of the cattle died on the way. It took about five months to reach Amaravati by foot. Only Manji Moti and a relative accompanied the livestock, and the rest of the family members travelled by train. They stay in forests with their cattle in tent houses about 10-15 kms away from Amaravati. They keep moving from one village to another almost once in every six months. They live in the company of many other Bharwaad families who have migrated similarly from other villages. Some of them return back to their villages after earning enough to take up some alternative livelihood.

Manji Moti's family has now 11 cows, 50 goats and 4 calves. Four cows are in milk yielding about 30 litres in a day. While about four litres are retained for family consumption, the rest is sold for cash income. Manji Moti and his second son, Gokul, graze the animals in the forests. Moti's first son, Jagga, collects milk from other migrant Bharwaads and supplies it to a private dairy. During peak season i.e. between October and May, he collects about 800 litres per day. The collection comes down to half during the lean period. The milk is sold at Rs. 7 per litre and Jagga gets a margin of Re. 1 per litre. Jagga owns a motorbike on which he carries milk. The money is paid by the dairy once in every ten days. Sometimes there could be delay even upto two months. Jagga has been pursuing this milk business in Amaravati for over five years.

Another source of income in Amaravati for the family is the night parking or folding of animals on farmers' land. Night parking is a way of manuring the land directly by parking an animal herd on the field. They get Rs. 200 for one night of parking depending upon whether the farmer has provided water to cattle or not. For about 4 months they are able to earn income from cattle parking by moving from farm to farm.

Migration to Amaravati no doubt has enabled Manji Moti's family to earn more than enough for livelihood survival. But the life itself has become one of real struggle and alienation. Living in the forest area, the family has to face constant harassment from the forest officials. Bribing or paying penalties for grazing the animals is a regular phenomenon. Moreover, being away from the native village with no information about the happenings in Bodiya, the family of Moti feels quite alienated. The family's visit to Bodiya during the festival season every year is only a small consolation for the long detachment. For Jagga's wife, Rupa, living in the forest area of Amaravati is a forced confinement. She would prefer to stay in Bodiya. Jagga is in a dilemma over whether to stay with his parents in Amaravati or move to Bodiya with his wife. Jagga's lucrative milk business would be the casualty in case he returns to Bodiya. Another worrying factor for the family is the education of the children which has suffered as a result of migration.

The family has a strong desire to return to Bodiya. Meanwhile, their unoccupied house in Bodiya had collapsed during rains in 1997. Jagga had a plan to start milk business in Bodiya similar to what he is doing in Amaravati. Despite some efforts, the plan did not fructify as he could not organize the collection of milk in the village.

Coupled with Jagga's failed attempt to start the milk business, a political stand-off between the Bharwaads and the other upper caste households had come in the way of Manji Moti's family even returning to the village temporarily for a year. In 1998, it was the turn of Manji Moti to graze the village cattle. The grazing would have fetched them an estimated income of Rs. 50,000 both in cash and kind. Disenchanted with the decision of the upper caste households not to support a Bharwaad woman candidate for the post of village sarpanch, the Bharwaad community had decided not to graze the animals of the upper caste during the year. At the same time, Jagga was also not all that keen to take up grazing in the village as he would be tied up for a year and not able to take up any other job.

Having escaped the uncertain livelihood in the village through migration, Manji Moti's family still has a deep desire to return to the village. The return, however, would depend upon the family pursuing a viable alternative occupation in the village. Till then, it is only continuation of the nomadic life and alienation for the family.

4.3 The Broader Livelihood Impact

A form of major local diversification that has taken place in Bodiya in recent decades is the agricultural modernisation and commercialization. Unlike in the past, Bodiya's agriculture is now dominated by cash crops, like cotton, sesame and cumin. These commercial crops now account for more than three-fourth of cropped area with cotton alone accounting for nearly 55 per cent of the total cropped area. The major crops grown in the village are cotton, sesame, bajra and jowar during kharif, and cumin, gram and wheat during rabi. Besides commercialisation, there is at the same time adoption of modern technology, though only partially, helping in improving the crop yields. Bajra is the major crop brought under high yielding varieties in a significant way. Use of chemical fertilizers is widespread, both across crops and farmers. Besides the adoption of new technology, the transformation of agriculture has been facilitated by investments in private wells and tractors by well-off farmers. Agriculture, overall, has got transformed from subsistence nature dependent on the vagaries of rainfall to a mechanised and commercialised nature partly insulated from rainfall uncertainty.

All these changes in agriculture have helped in increasing crop yields and incomes of the land owning class. These changes also have enabled them to acquire new income earning avenues like selling water and hiring out tractor services. The huge investment in irrigation by the well-off has enabled them to get access to common pool resources like groundwater and utilise them for pure private gains.

The gains from agricultural commercialisation and mechanisation apart, the well-off among Patels, Darbaars, Dalwaadis and Koli Patels, have consolidated their positions further by securing government jobs, opening diamond polishing units, and pursuing trade and business in the village. In all the above ventures, the landed class in general, and Patels, in particular, have been greatly benefited by remittances from members of their families who have migrated to cities mainly for pursuing diamond polishing. Overall, the impact of the above diversification for the well-off has been highly positive in terms of higher incomes, better education for children, better housing and improved capacity for risk bearing and entrepreneurial ventures.

The middle strata, while also benefiting from agricultural commercialisation has tried to broaden its livelihood base by pursuing agricultural labour work, trade and business and diamond polishing work both within and outside the village. Certain women specific diversification also could be observed among these households. The spinning activity pursued almost exclusively by the women of the Darbaar caste and the skilled embroidery work by young women belonging to the Dalwaadi community are two such examples.

The nature of diversification in the case of those pursuing traditional occupations presents a picture of their struggle against the forces of development and change. The diversification strategies of two such communities like the Bharwaads and Kumbhaars are worth mentioning here. Bharwaads are traditionally dependent on cattle rearing. With the declining water and fodder availability in the village, the Bharwaads have been compelled to reduce their livestock strength. A number of Bharwaad households have migrated to far-off places to secure water and fodder for their livestock and market for their products. Some of their men folk have taken up diamond polishing work in the village. Similarly, Kumbhaars, the traditional potters, faced with a situation of declining demand for pottery and the dilemma of sustaining a traditional occupation, have been compelled to pursue occupations like diamond polishing to supplement their livelihood. Even among the traditional communities, those with relatively better abilities have been able to take up self-employment ventures like flour mill, tailoring work, and small transportation. However, one can see the continuation of certain traditional occupations like blacksmith and carpentry pursued by Lohaars. There is a continued demand for these services with some upgradation of technology being done.

The forces of diversification have also impacted households in the lower rungs of the socio-economic order in Bodiya. These are households belonging to Vaaghri, Pagi and Bhangi castes who are mostly landless or own only very little land. The agricultural intensification has helped them in terms of increased labour employment within the village. A few of them supplement their livelihoods by diamond polishing work, petty trade, fuelwood and charcoal sale, etc. Two policy initiatives which have helped these sections in overcoming their vulnerability partly are the distribution of small pieces of village wasteland for agriculture to landless and providing small government jobs under the policy of reservation. As such, the poors have not been able to diversify and benefit in a major way like the well-off categories. Though in absolute terms the poor households have obtained some benefits from the diversification process, many of them still remain in abject poverty and vulnerable conditions. This was evident from the adverse impact of the flash flood that was seen in Bodiya in 1997. While the well-off households with good housing were unaffected; the landless and lower caste households living in the periphery had their houses severely damaged with some of them being rendered even houseless temporarily.

5. CONCLUSION

To conclude, Bodiya, a semi-arid village, exhibits occupational diversification of a significant nature and magnitude. All sections of the village have diversified either to supplement the earnings from their primary or traditional occupations or to widen the opportunities for economic consolidation and accumulation. However, one can see a wide variation both in the form and impact of diversification across different sections because of the differences in the household resource endowments. What are noticeable besides the changes in the occupational structure are the changes that have taken place in agriculture in recent decades by way of increased farm intensity, adoption of new technology and growing commercialisation reducing some of the previous vulnerabilities. Though the benefits of agricultural changes have reached all sections including the landless, the major gains have been garnered by those in upper rungs of the socio-economic hierarchy. In the non-farm sector, diamond polishing has emerged as the dominant form of diversification helping a large section especially those in the upper and middle strata to supplement their livelihood from agriculture. Unable to gain fully from the above changes because of many socio-economic disadvantages, the poors have been compelled to diversify in distress. As a result, while the rich have been able to further consolidate their position through diversification, the poors have been able to only manage their survival, at times even repenting over the nature of their diversification. What emerges from Bodiya is diversification of a varied nature leading to further accentuation of the existing socio-economic divide.

That apart, diversification in Bodiya also displays the dimension of external dependence similar to what is observed in Mahudi and Mahunala. Growing external dependence could be seen in diamond polishing and in some service activities. Diamond polishing which has emerged as a major form of diversification is highly dependent on external sources both for its existence and continuation. The external dependence of diamond polishing also has a strong urban linkage and influence. The nature of this external linkage of diversification observed in the study villages is examined in more details in the next chapter.

5

DIVERSIFICATION AND RURAL-URBAN LINKAGES

1. INTRODUCTION

The analysis in the previous two chapters has brought out clearly the existence of a strong urban linkage in the occupational diversification process that has taken place in semi-arid villages like Mahudi, Mahunala and Bodiya. Although the households are diversifying into different activities based both in rural and urban areas, at the same time, one can observe the dominance of occupations having strong links with urban areas and in specific labour intensive industries. In the case of Mahudi and Mahunala, an overwhelming proportion of the migrant households pursue construction activity of various kinds. Over the years, they have almost come to specialize as unskilled construction and road workers. The massive growth of construction industry with increased demand for unskilled workers seems to have facilitated the absorption, in large numbers, of migrants from villages like Mahudi and Mahunala. Similarly, in Bodiya a large proportion of households have diversified into activities such as diamond polishing having strong urban links. Diamond polishing is pursued both in the urban and rural areas. Its growth in the rural areas can be traced to strong socio-economic links established with the urban areas by the migrants over the years.

Understanding this urban linkage of rural occupational diversification becomes important for many reasons. As identified in Chapter 2, studies focusing on the urban facet of diversification would help in assessing the impact of the process of urbanization on rural poverty. Second, by such studies one can get clearly an understanding of the functioning of the labour markets both in the rural and urban areas. Based on the insights about the functioning of labour markets, one can analyse how urbanisation creates demand for rural labour and explore to what extent rural labour stand to gain in the process given the terms and conditions of such employment. Third, the understanding would also help in addressing the broader question of how far such rural and urban linkages would help in attaining a balanced rural-urban growth.

The present chapter makes an attempt to address some of the above issues of rural-urban linkages focusing specifically on the two dominant diversified activities, viz., construction activity and the diamond polishing pursued by the households in the study villages. More than examining these two activities *per se,* what is attempted mainly in the chapter is to understand their emergence as a source for rural livelihood diversification, the scope available for income and employment generation, and the nature of working and living conditions of those engaged in these two activities.

The present chapter consists of four sections including the present Section. Section 2 deals with the nature of construction activity as pursued by migrants from Mahudi and Mahunala. Section 3 makes an attempt to explain the phenomenon of circulatory migration observed in the case of migrant households. Section 4 deals with the nature of diamond polishing activity as observed in the case of Bodiya. Section 5 draws briefly conclusions based on the overall analysis in the chapter.

2. ROLE OF CONSTRUCTION INDUSTRY IN RURAL OCCUPATION DIVERSIFICATION

Given the dominance of construction work among various activities pursued by the migrants from Mahudi and Mahunala, an attempt is made in this section to understand the nature of construction activity and the living and working conditions of migrants involved in this activity. The analysis is based on the data collected both in the study villages and at some of places of destination of the migration like Surat, Ahmedabad, Anand and Nadiad.

In the current model of development, construction industry is considered as one of the 'big three' of development along with transportation and energy industry. Construction forms the essence of what planners term as development, directly or indirectly, as it touches the life of every household. The construction industry plays an important role in the socio-economic development especially in generating employment for the labour force. In a developing country like India, the intensity of construction activity is even regarded as an indicator of the economic growth.

Construction work is perennial in nature and hence provides substantial employment opportunities. There is high demand for unskilled, semi-skilled and skilled workers in the construction industry. Of all the industries, construction recorded the highest annual average growth rate employment of 7.1 per cent during 1994-2000 in the country (Government of India, 2002). The number of people employed in this industry is also quite significant with construction accounting for 7.4 per cent of the total workforce employed in the country during 1999-2000 (*ibid.*). The construction industry can be divided broadly into two segments: housing construction and infrastructure and turnkey projects like roads, civic amenities, dams and commercial and administrative buildings. At any time, the housing construction is affected by two factors, the price of the real estate and the availability of the credit in the system. The government policies and investments, on the other hand, influence greatly infrastructural projects. During recession the construction industry is also among the hardest hit industries. But many have long regarded public works as an ideal sponge for soaking up the unemployed workers in the economy. The construction industry is bound to gain further momentum. This is due to the continued growth in the country's population, fast pace of urbanisation, new policies of the government encouraging private investments in the sector and easy housing finance schemes of banks and financial institutions. It is in various types of construction activities mentioned above that one can find the large scale employment of migrant labourers from rural areas.

Labour Market

As could be observed in the case of migrants from Mahudi and Mahunala almost all of them work as unskilled casual labourers in various types of construction activities. The major channel of employment for the migrants is the casual labour markets. One can find labour markets with varying sizes functioning in every city or town for construction work. The modes of operations in all these labour markets are very similar. The construction labourers get together in these markets to find employment, while the contractors and other employers also come to these markets to find labourers. To understand the *modus operandi* of these markets, we looked at one such labour market in Surat known locally as Balashram market. The Balashram labour market is one of the four such markets functioning in Surat. It is operative from 7 a.m. in the morning when both the workers and the contractors start assembling. Not less than 600 construction workers assemble at this market on any day during summer. All the daily wage casual labourers and even some of the labourers who have struck a long-term contract come to the labour market every day. While the daily wage casual labourers come to get a job; the other labourers come there to be picked up to reach the work place. As such there are no middlemen involved in this market and the negotiations are held directly between the workers and the contractors. The migrants from Dahod and other neighbouring districts dominate the labour market. Most of these migrants work in groups. The male members go and strike a deal, while the female companions wait for them. The deals are normally struck for the entire group with a contractor. Given the high demand for casual workers in various types of construction work, all the migrants normally get picked up. The prevailing wage rate during the summer of 1998 was Rs 70 per day for the unskilled workers. Work is also taken up on a piece-rate basis for which very hard bargaining takes place. If the workplace is far off, then the contractor gives the workers transportation cost for reaching the work place. The migrants generally tend to look for contractors who are familiar to them as they do not want to face any difficulties during work in terms of the nature of the work and the wage promised at the time of the deal.

What is also interesting to observe in the labour market is that given a competitive kind of wage rate, which prevailed in this labour market, there are all possibilities for the market to get cleared. But what we observed was that the labour market clearance actually does not always take place which is not due to excess labour supply. There are many reasons for some of the labour force in the market not getting absorbed on a particular day. One, at times labourers prefer short duration jobs wherein the minimum living cost of the day is covered. Many labourers prefer to undertake such jobs after having worked continuously for a long period of time. Instead of taking a day off, they try to get some work. Second, the workers do not accept certain tasks as they are very strenuous and involve long hours of labour even though high wage rate may be paid.

Working Conditions

The conditions of work for the unskilled casual labourers in the construction industry are found to be quite harsh. Though there is a high demand for labour of all kinds there is no job security or permanency. No rules and regulations pertaining to employment are being implemented and labour laws seem to be followed more in violation. These labourers are unaware of their principal employer as there is a chain of contractors between the principal employer and them. Very rarely one finds labourers permanently working under one contractor. The permanent employer-employee relationship is very rarely established thereby denying the benefits of social welfare legislations available to these labourers.

The industry comprises of highly specified tasks. For each task and stage a different contractor is engaged and under each contractor different labourers are working. All construction labourers are casual workers. No time limit is fixed to make payments to the labourers. In many cases an advance is made to meet their consumption needs and the wages are paid only after the contract is finished. This mechanism assures uninterrupted supply of labour for the contractor to complete the work. This kind of an advance system prevails for both skilled and unskilled workers. The skilled workers are paid on a monthly or a fortnightly basis and there were also complaints of non-payment of wages.

Construction activity has been covered by the Government of Gujarat for the implementation of Minimum Wages Act. Under the Act, labourers are divided into three categories as per their skills; skilled, semi-skilled and unskilled. But almost all the labourers are covered under skilled or unskilled category. It was found that contractors do not pay wages as per the Minimum Wages Act (Pandya, 1993). The minimum wages paid to the labourers consist of the basic wage and special allowance. The special allowance is linked with the cost of living index and is revised and declared in the months of April and October. The minimum wages of labourers are changed at the interval of every six months. But what we found in the case of construction labourers was that the wages were fixed by contractors either on the basis of time or piece-rate and were not revised with the revision of the minimum wages.

The wages were being determined largely by the availability of the labourers at the labour market and the demand for labourers at the construction site. At the time of Diwali and Holi festivals when construction work is at its peak and the labour supply is less, wage rates are slightly increased during this period. Holi and Diwali are also an important festival occasions for the tribals besides partly being the period of their peak agricultural operations. During the winter season there is a reverse situation. As a large number of tribals migrate to various urban centres seeking employment in the construction activity, there is a lowering of the wage rates.

Further, under the Minimum Wages Act, it is obligatory to issue an attendance card to each and every labourer. But none of the workers were found in possession of these cards. There was also the violation of the provision of Equal Remuneration Act, as women labourers are normally paid five to ten rupees less than the male labourers for the same work. There are no fixed working hours and usually labourers are working for eight to ten hours per day. They do not get paid for overtime particularly when employed for private works. In the case of public construction work, the contractors sometimes pay overtime wage for extra working hours. Being largely unaware of overtime wage, the labourers do not demand the same.

In the case of labourers who stay at the construction sites though they get regular employment but again do not get wages as per the Minimum Wages Act. This is because the contractors normally in the pretext of providing regular jobs neither pay minimum wages nor provide any other facilities in the work place like shelter, drinking water, toilet facility and light.

The construction work also involves high degree of risk and danger. It proceeds even under scorching heat or rainy weather or at odd times in a day. Accidents are also common as most of the operations are carried out with inadequate safety measures. In Mahudi, a family reported the death of a young woman while working in a building construction site. Similarly, in Mahunala a labourer reported that he discontinued migration due to serious burn injury to his hands suffered during a road construction. There is neither a proper enforcement of safety measures by the authorities nor payment of adequate compensation to the victims of such accidents. In addition to these dangers, due to continuous exposure to heat and dust workers face many health hazards like irritation of lungs and eyes, skin diseases and high blood pressure. A member of a case study household in Mahudi who was working as a skilled mason had developed a serious skin allergy in his hands. With the result, he now works only as an unskilled labourer.

Living Conditions

Visits to the living places of the migrants revealed that the migrant labourers, particularly, those involved in various construction work do not have any proper housing facilities. One could find them living on construction sites or in open spaces like a vacant housing plot, road sides, unoccupied buildings or even on platforms of railway and bus stations. An analysis of the living conditions of migrant households from the village Mahudi showed that members of 82 per cent of the households lived in open places (Table 5.1); most of them involved in construction activity. The living conditions of these migrants were dismal with miserable existence. Their life seemed to be very harsh when compared to their villages. They were exposed to open air during all the seasons with no roof to protect themselves. The migrant workers normally carry minimal clothing and other belongings. They have absolutely no sanitation and drinking water available at their place of stay. They travel long distances to fetch water from a public place or a private residence or from the construction site. They went for defecation in the open places either in the late times of the night or early mornings. Many stay with their women and children for weeks together under such conditions.

Table 5.1
Living Places of the Migrants

(No. of households)

Activity	*Rented*	*Open Place*	*Factory Premises*	*Total*
Construction Work	1	18	-	19
Truck Loading	-	10	-	10
Glass Factory	-	-	4	4
Agriculture Labour	-	3	-	3
Total	1 (2.63)	31 (81.58)	4 (15.79)	36 (100.0)

Source: Based on Field Survey in Mahudi, 1997.
N.B.: Figures in brackets are percentages to total.
Con. = Construction. Agr. = Agriculture.

The migrants when they come to the cities normally live in groups of varying sizes. Migrants of same kinship try to inhabit at a particular place. This suggests a mechanism by which such groups develop defence mechanism against a possible hostile urban environment by replicating the structure they leave behind. This ensures peer groups and kin living together. It also makes it easy to continuously keep contacts with their families back home, sending money to them; borrow from known people at times of crisis and supporting a new entrant till he is put on a job.

In open places, the living space of these migrants is demarked by a hedge in which their grain bags, a pot for drinking water, cooking utensils and bedsheets are safe-guarded. Sometimes stray animals eat away the grain or flour as the goods are unguarded. The migrants normally bring maize with them, which would last for few days. They buy their other daily essentials like spices, oil and fuelwood from the nearby shops.

Only the labourers who stayed at construction sites had slightly better amenities as they could live either in the building under construction or use some sheets or building material which then served as roof. Some of these migrants could get access to water facility on the construction site.

These deplorable conditions of living continue to persist inspite of the stipulation of the Section 17 of the Contract Labour Act. The Act stipulates that within 15 days of the commencement of the employment of contract labourers, the contractors are obliged to provide rest rooms or other suitable alternative accommodations at every place where the labour is required to halt at night in connection with the work and in which employment is likely to continue for three months or more.

Thus, though there is assured employment for the unskilled migrant workers in the construction industry but the living and working conditions are found to be quite harsh. The employment is casual fragmented by contract and sub-contract resulting in highly adverse term for the workers. None of the basic labour laws seem to have come to their help forcing them to lead a life of squalor.

3. CIRCULATORY MOVEMENT OF LABOUR : AN EXPLANATION

The phenomenon of seasonal migration observed in the case of villages like Mahudi and Mahunala display highly circulatory character. Migrants from this region move constantly from villages to cities and from cities back to their villages making the migration to assume a circulatory form. The general pattern of migration is that the labour force moves out soon after the harvesting of kharif crop and sowing for the rabi season is completed. The migration period is spread over a period of about 6 to 8 months from

November to June. Though the migrants keep travelling between the city and their village many times during the migration period, they finally return on the onset of monsoon to start the new agricultural season. This pattern of migration has been continuing for the last few decades and has become a permanent feature of labour force movement prevailing in this region. Similar circulatory pattern of unskilled labour movement has been observed in many other parts of the country (Jagnnathan and Halder 1988; de Haan 1997). Given such a pattern, some of the questions that arise are: why are these migrants following such a circulatory pattern of migration ? What are the constraints preventing them to migrate permanently to cities, particularly when the duration of migration is found to be for a longer period? What are the forces pushing or pulling them back to their villages? Whether the harsh living and working conditions of these migrants in cities, as depicted above, are in any way influencing the pattern? An attempt is made in this section to address some of the above questions and thereby find an explanation to the phenomenon of circulatory migration adopted by the Bhil migrants pursuing construction work in cities.

The insights gained from the interactions we had with the migrants reveal that there are factors operating at both ends of migration which push and pull these migrants between their villages and cities. Diagram 5.1 using the Nine-Square Mandala approach to livelihood presents the factors influencing the phenomenon of circulatory migration. The Nine-Square Mandala, as explained in Chapter 1, depicts the livelihood system of a household or of a community as having nine dimensional focus which relate to various material and non-material realities of life. Each of the nine squares represents one of the nine realities of livelihood identified by the approach. For seasonal migrants in a sense there exist two livelihood systems, rural and urban, as depicted in the Diagram 5.1. The prominent factors relating to various livelihood realities influencing the migration

Diagram 5.1: The Push and Pull Factors of Circulatory Migration

Rural Livelihood		
9. Individual Orientation *-Peasant Identity*	8. Family Orientation	7. Collective Orientation
6. Inner Human Space	5. Family Space *-Own house*	4. Socio-economic Space *- Kinship/Bride price & Chandlavidhi*
3. Emotional Base *-Attachment to land & village*	2. Knowledge of Activity Base *-Low literacy and skills*	1. Physical Base *- Small land-holding*

Pull ⟷ Push   Pull ⟷ Push

Urban Livelihood		
9. Individual Orientation *- No Clear identity*	8. Family Orientation	7. Collective Orientation
6. Inner Human Space	5. Family Space *-Live in open places*	4. Socio-economic Space *-Absence of Social Network*
3. Emotional Base	2. Knowledge & Activity Base *-Casual unskilled labour*	1. Physical Base *-Growing Construction Activity*

NB: The factors given in italics are the key variables identified under the respective square or livelihood dimension influencing the circulatory migration.

pattern have been identified and plotted in the relevant squares of the two Mandalas representing the rural and the urban livelihood systems of the migrants. These factors put together are found to be simultaneously pushing and pulling the migrants between their villages and cities resulting in their migration acquiring a circulatory character.

As analysed in Chapter 3, distress condition arising out of the inability to sustain the livelihood with limited local resource base is the major reason pushing the households to migrate to cities looking for supplementary sources of income and employment. Besides, there is also the need for additional income to meet social obligations like payment of bride price and contribution to *chandlavidhi* which forces households to resort to migration. Given the low level of literacy and skills possessed by them, there is hardly any kind of choice other than getting absorbed in low paid jobs available in the unorganised sector. It is here that the booming construction industry with the potential to absorb the unskilled labour force on a large scale has come in quite handy for migrants from villages like Mahudi and Mahunala. The work in the construction industry goes on mainly during winter and summer season overlapping largely with the lean periods of these migrants in their villages. Also most migrants, both female and male, seem to prefer the construction work as not only there is a surety of employment but also it gives them enough flexibility to switch from migration to farm work and vice versa as and when needed.

At the same time, the construction industry cannot provide employment to such unskilled labour force throughout the year. Nor are there other activities in cities which can absorb such unskilled workers on a large scale. Therefore, the chances for the migrants to get a year long sustained employment are limited even if they are keen to work. Further, not many among the migrants have been able to acquire newer skills either to move up the ladder in the job market or to get absorbed in other occupations. Thus, their limited skills and the type of employment available to them become a major constraint to stay for a longer period in the cities.

The dismal living conditions of migrants, as observed in the previous section, is another reason which really creates a feeling of dejection forcing them to return to the comforts of their villages often during the period of migration. The migrants have to put up with highly inhuman living conditions in cities as they live mostly in open spaces having no protection and basic amenities. Migration during rainy season hence is ruled out for most. Again they have to move frequently from one living place to another depending upon the location of work or when the open site in which they live gets cleared for some new construction. This also forces them to carry very little of supporting things like clothes, vessels and beddings. The living conditions worsen further when the women and young children accompany the male migrants to cities. As a coping strategy, many migrants leave women and children back at home, especially during winter season as living in the open places becomes really difficult.

Given the low wages and also the prime intention of carrying back home most of the income earned, hardly any migrant can afford to take up a house on rent even for a very modest living. Only a very few migrants working in factories or with building contractors on a more regular basis were found having some accommodation for living. Such migrants were also found to be living in cities for a longer duration as compared to those who lived in open and unprotected places.

Apart from the harsh working and living conditions pushing the migrants to return back to their villages, we could also identify some socio-psychological reasons driving them back to the villages.

The Bhils who migrate to cities as casual unskilled labourers and live in absolute dismal conditions, are back home peasants owning and cultivating land though their holdings are small. Having been reduced to mere casual labourers in cities, they possess a strong urge to retain their self-image of being peasants. Any attempt to stay back longer in cities will be at the cost of foregoing their primary occupation which gives them the peasant identity. Being aware of the fact that life in the cities does not bestow them with any identity, the Bhils return to their native villages to actualize their self-image. In the cities, the Bhils are an object of ridicule for the locals. The Bhil migrants are called derogatively as *mamo log* (one meaning being relatives who come looking for hospitality) in many places of their migration. There is, thus, a strong sense of detest towards the city life and an equally strong emotional attachment towards the village. The urge for the Bhils is to live and thrive in their own villages than in cities bereft of any self-image. The aim of earnings from the cities is merely to supplement their livelihood in the village.

Further, leaving the village permanently in search of greener pastures in cities is a move which is socially counter productive for a Bhil. First of all, such a move would invite social castigation from the village community. Those leaving the village would be rebuked for their desperate action. Secondly, even if somebody decides to settle down in cities, the absence of any kinship network would pose problems in finding suitable marriage alliances for their children. In the current context, a meaningful social life for the Bhils becomes possible only if they live in the midst of their community than in the social vacuum of cities.

Thus, a complex set of factors which fall in both economic and non-economic spheres of livelihood are found to be influencing the phenomenon of return migration of the Bhils. The phenomenon, thus, is an outcome of the existing socio-economic milieu of the Bhils. As long as the milieu remains the same, the phenomenon is likely to continue in the same form. This is captured in the following case of a household migrating to the city of Anand for the last twenty years but still refusing to settle down permanently.

Sticking to the Roots: The Case of Mangal Singh

To stick to one's roots is certainly what Marcel Mauss called 'total social fact' (quoted in Racine 1997). The motivations behind such a choice, although apparently simple, are in fact very complex as a number of considerations—social, economic, cultural, psychological, are at play. What perhaps provides immense security for a tribal community like the Bhils are the family and kinship ties and customs and traditions which instil a sense of belongingness besides giving some identity to an individual in the village. Being a member of a society means a bestowal of a social identity that gets obliterated or at least becomes hazy, when one moves out to a different place.

Combined with these factors is the existence of an emotional tie with the land and the dwelling. A strong force apparently binds an individual to his or her farm land. It is the land that provides food and the livelihood *per se* revolves around land. This sense of binding to one's roots becomes very obvious from the case of Mangal Singh, a Bhil seasonal migrant labour.

Mangal Singh belongs to Jessavada village which is in the Dahod district. He has been migrating to Anand continuously for the past twenty years. He was young and unmarried when he started migrating. As in any semi-arid tracts, the farmers in Dahod also face the problem of erratic and irregular rainfall. Mangal Singh is able to raise two dry crops on his land. The farming does not need intensive labour and there is sufficient surplus labour available during the year. The surplus labour in the family is able to migrate during the lean agricultural periods. However, the need to migrate primarily arises as the land is not able to produce adequate food for sustaining the livelihood in the village.

Mangal Singh along with his family members works with a building contractor in Anand for almost eight months in a year and only during the peak agricultural season the family returns to the village. He has been working with this contractor for the last ten years. In Anand they stay in a small one room house provided to them by the contractor on his factory premises. They go home during Akhatri, Diwali and Holi festivals for sowing and harvesting of crops and to attend marriages.

Mangal Singh has six children, four daughters and two sons. His eldest child is a daughter who is 18 years old and his youngest child is a one-year old son. In the initial years of his migration as an unskilled construction labourer he would earn about Rs. 1.50 per day. In the last twenty years he has worked in the construction of buildings for many prominent institutions at Anand. In between he went to Balasinor, a small town in Anand district, for three years to work in the construction of a health centre. Mangal Singh who started as an unskilled labourer has slowly learnt the trade and has now become a skilled worker. As a skilled worker he earns about Rs. 80 per day, while the female members of his family who work as unskilled labourers earn about Rs. 40 per day. Mangal Singh earns about Rs. 3000 per month and his wife and daughter who work along with him, earn about Rs. 1000 each. In all, they are able to earn about Rs. 5000 per month. They spend about Rs. 900 for transport as they commute from their place of stay. They spend about Rs. 1500 on food and other expenses and are able to save about Rs. 2500 per month.

During his three years of stay in Balasinor while constructing the health centre he was offered a piece of land to construct a house of his own so that he could stay and continue with his occupation. But he did not accept it. Mangal Singh did not want to invest in constructing a house far away from his village. Instead, he preferred to build a house in his own village. Also he found living in Balasinor unsafe because of robbery. Similarly, he has also found Anand to be a costly place to settle down and he would not be able to afford buying or constructing a house.

This apart, there was a fear in him that his native villagers would ridicule his family for trying to construct a house elsewhere without caring about the native house and land. As Leelaben, Mangal Singh's wife, put it they would have been called *bikaris* (beggars) if they were to settle down elsewhere permanently leaving behind their village. Moreover city life is devoid of kinship and other social attachments present in the native village. If they settle down in the migrant place it would become very difficult to get their girls married. Hence to Mangal Singh and his family retaining the linkage with the native village is of paramount importance.

Further, Mangal Singh is the eldest of the three brothers and his mother lives with him in the village. His first younger brother is also a seasonal migrant who works as a construction labourer in Anand. His second brother works as a watchman in Godhra.

The land which they own in the village is under the joint ownership of all the three brothers. The family owns about 45 acres of land. They have two houses, one of them is built by their parents in which the families of the two younger brothers live. The other house is the new one built by Mangal Singh about five years back investing about rupees one lakh. All the money for constructing the house was earned from migration.

Mangal Singh and his family members identify themselves with their village where they have their lands, house and family ties. For them, Anand is just a place of work and there is no emotional attachment with it. As Mangal Singh said, 'I am born in Jessavada and I have to be buried in Jessavada'.

This shows that the socio-cultural and psychological reasons like the ties of blood and self-identity make the Bhils develop a strong attachment to their place of birth. Culturally, an individual acquires a number of traits during the process of socialization that have a lot of bearing on family's well-being in a given social context. In the psychic realm, the decision of an individual to resort to a circulatory kind of migration instead of permanent migration springs from factors relating to pride and fear. The pride is that of actualising the peasant identity and fear is that of being ridiculed by neighbours for not remaining in the native to be able to tend the land.

The emotional attachment to land comes from the fact that it has been inherited from their forefathers. It is a source of livelihood not only for the present but also for future generation. In the event of their children failing to get a job outside, the family land would remain as the main support for livelihood. Another factor is the reverence that is shown to the animals which help in their agriculture and other pursuits. There is no way animals could be ignored because of migration. To get away from this entire milieu is not an easy task for a migrant.

The case of Mangal Singh, thus, illustrates that economic rationale alone cannot explain a migrant's behaviour. There is no exclusive choice between economics and psychology. In other words, as is argued, the laws of society are not necessarily those of the market place even though the markets cover the whole of society.

4. ROLE OF DIAMOND POLISHING IN BODIYA

This section makes an attempt to look at the nature of diamond polishing activity in the village Bodiya mainly in terms of its genesis, magnitude, entrepreneurship and generation of income and employment opportunities. In examining all this, the main aim is to trace the influence of urban linkage in the emergence of the activity as a source of livelihood for households in rural areas.

Genesis

Among the many diversified occupations found in Bodiya, diamond polishing is the most prominent one. A large number of households are involved in diamond polishing activity. Diamond polishing activity has come to play an important role in supporting the livelihood in Bodiya which is primarily dependent on rainfed farming. Currently, diamond polishing is one of the leading export-oriented industries in the country. The gems and jewellery industry which also includes diamond polishing activity accounted for about 16 to 20 per cent of the total value of country's exports in recent years (Government of India, 2002). Gujarat is the leading State which accounts for bulk of the exports. Though in Bodiya, the first diamond polishing unit was set up only after 1980, the people of Bodiya have been involved in diamond polishing activity at least from 1970 onwards.

Saurashtra region, where Bodiya is located, has been one of the chronic drought affected regions in Gujarat. The region has experienced many severe droughts in the past. Going by the account given by the elders, migration, both permanent and temporary, has been one of the major coping strategies of the people against drought. The city of Surat in South Gujarat is one of the major destinations of the migrants from the region. By late 1960s, the diamond industry had spread from the Mumbai to Surat. For the migrants from Saurashtra, diamond polishing became one of the major sources of employment. Gradually, some of the migrants even moved up to become big businessmen and entrepreneurs in the diamond industry. The Saurashtrians who have set up diamond polishing units in Surat have encouraged their own kinsmen from native villages to come and work for them (Engelshoven 1999). As recalled by a group of elderly persons in Bodiya, the first person, who migrated to Surat for diamond polishing work, was a Patel by caste. He went there on the invitation of his relative who was already there in the diamond business. The same person, as recalled by elders, later on went on to become a prosperous man in Surat by pursuing diamond business. By 1975, a large number of such people had migrated to Surat looking for fortune in the diamond business. According to a villager, when the diamond industry was hit by a recession during 1975-76 many were rendered jobless and had to return back to their villages selling off their belongings in Surat.

Over the years, the diamond industry has spread from Surat to other cities and towns like Ahmedabad, Rajkot, Bhavnagar and Botad in Gujarat. Many people from rural areas have migrated permanently to these centres. In Bodiya itself we could observe that more than 25 households have migrated permanently to cities like Surat and Ahmedabad in the last two and half decades to pursue diamond polishing work. Interestingly, most of these households are from the Patel caste which is indicative of the influence of kinship factor in determining such migration. As discussed earlier, most of these migrants have built their own houses in these cities and reside with their kith and kin. Many of them send regular remittances back home and also receive their shares of agricultural produce. The members of these households visit the village during festivals and other social occasions. Back in the village, these permanent migrants are still considered as residents of Bodiya. It is this link established through migration to cities, which has played a major role in the emergence of diamond polishing units even in the village.

Magnitude

The households in Bodiya pursue diamond polishing both within and outside the village. Within the village many diamond polishing units have come up in the last one and half decades providing employment opportunity for the local workforce. People are found involved in diamond work in three ways, as owners of polishing units, as workers and as traders though only a very few pursue trading. Over 90 per cent of the people are involved in diamond polishing as workers.

As per the household survey about 55 per cent of the households in the village are engaged in this activity. Among the households involved in diamond polishing, while in about 50 per cent of the cases, members of households work only within the village; in about 25 per cent cases members migrate out. In the rest of the 25 per cent cases, members work both within and outside the village. Overall, in about 50 per cent of the households pursuing diamond polishing members migrate for diamond work.

In terms of total labour force in the village, diamond polishing accounts for about 31 per cent of the total. Those who migrate for diamond work alone account for about 63 per cent of the seasonal migrant labour force of Bodiya. Thus, the magnitude of diamond polishing both in terms of the households covered and the labour force employed is quite significant. However, as discussed in Chapter 4 it is mainly the households belonging to upper and middle castes who have taken up diamond polishing. Among the lower castes, only a very few are found involved in it. Though the members from lower castes mentioned that as such there is no barrier for them to get involved in diamond polishing work but still the spread has been found to be very low among the lower castes. Similarly, in terms of gender, the labour force is almost entirely dominated by male workers. Only very recently, a few women from Kumbhar and Koli Patel castes have taken up diamond polishing work in the village.

Village Entrepreneurship

At the time of the study, there were five entrepreneurs running diamond polishing units in Bodiya. The number of units varied in the village with frequent entry and exit of entrepreneurs. The units are of varying size. Of the five diamond polishing unit owners, two each belonged to Patel and Koli Patel castes, and one to Dalwadi caste (Table 5.2). The local entrepreneurs are all from the upper and middle social strata of the village. Interestingly, all of them in the past were involved in diamond polishing either as a trader or as a labourer in towns. At the same time, some of them have close contact or relationship with those in diamond business outside the village. It is this past experience and

Table 5.2
Some Details of Diamond Polishing Entrepreneurs in Bodiya

Sr. No.	*Entrepreneur*	*Year of starting*	*Caste*	*Past expe-rience*	*Source of capital*	*No. of Machi-nes*	*No. of work-ers*
1.	Magan Takarsi	1984	Patel	Brother was DP Trader	DP Trader	1 L, 2 P	9
2.	Ganshyam-bhai	1994	Koli Patel	DP worker	DP Trader and Friends	–	26
3.	Nanji Jagjivan	1997	Koli Patel	DP worker	DP Trader, Own Capital and Loan	4 L, 5 P	15-28
4.	Sonda Darmasi	–	Dal-wadi	DP worker	Own capital and Loan	3 L*, 1 P	5

Source : Household Survey in Bodiya. Detailed information could not be collected for the fifth unit.
* Lathes are located outside the village.
L = Lathe, P = Polishing Wheel, DP = Diamond Polishing

the contact which has greatly helped these entrepreneurs to start diamond polishing units in the village. Besides such a linkage, an over-riding economic reason also has played a major role in the spread of diamond processing activity in the rural areas of Saurashtra including village Bodiya. The diamonds which are processed in villages like Bodiya are of inferior quality. They are primarily wastes or rejects of bigger diamond processing centres in cities like Surat and Ahmedabad which handle diamonds of higher quality. For the units located in cities, processing such lower quality diamond would be uneconomical given the relatively higher labour cost. Since there is also an alternative market for smaller diamonds made out of the rejects, the crucial thing would be to get the rejects processed at a cheaper cost. Given the availability of cheap labour in rural areas, the diamond traders in cities seem to have found it attractive to tap this cheap labour. The traders have encouraged with necessary financial support, those interested in opening diamond polishing units in villages. It is here the contact possessed by the rural entrepreneurs mentioned above has become crucial for the traders to approach them. In Bodiya, of the five entrepreneurs, four have received financial help from such traders for their ventures besides mobilising part of the capital on their own.

While two of the owners run their units in worksheds built exclusively for the diamond work; the others operate their units in their own residential premises. The main earning for the owners of these units is the commission they receive from the traders on each diamond processed in their units. For every diamond, the owners of the unit get a commission of one rupee. The total earnings of the unit owners would, therefore, depend upon the number of diamonds they are able to process which in turn depends on the number of lathes and rotating machines they possess and the number of labourers they are able to employ. The number of such machines owned in the diamond polishing units of Bodiya varied from three to nine; and the number of labourers employed from five to twenty eight. The monthly income of the owners from diamond polishing varied from Rs. 1,000 to Rs. 13,000.

Process

The entire process of diamond polishing in the village goes on in the following way:

The owners of the units first contact diamond traders in places like Surat, Ahmedabad and Limdi. They deposit a sum of money varying between 80 to 90 per cent of the diamond value with the traders and promise to shape and polish the diamonds by a certain date. The agreed quantity of raw material arrives through local couriers called *angadias* who come with clear specifications about weight and value of diamonds. They hand over the raw material to the unit owners and promise to return by a certain date with the needed money for making payments to labourers. The owners then organise the labourers and allocates tasks based on their skills.

The raw materials of unpolished diamonds is given in a measure of carats which could vary in value from Rs. 200 per carat to Rs. 2,000 per carat depending upon the quality. A carat typically consists of 45 small or 15 big pieces of diamonds. Each piece is called a *nag*. The note accompanying the raw materials provides the number of carats and the value associated with them.

The first step is the removal of extraneous particles like coal, dust and mud from the diamonds. This is done on mechanised lathes and the workers using a magnifying glass continuously inspect the diamonds. This task is tedious as it requires great skill in handling the diamond and adjusting the lathe to the right speed and friction. The lathe worker also needs to bear in mind the specifications sent by the trader. The traders normally specify the percentage of impurities by weight present in the raw materials despatched. This varies between 50 to 70 per cent of the total weight of the raw material. The lathe worker has to ensure that the cleaning of the diamond does not reduce its weight below 30 per cent of the original weight. If the weight of a cleaned diamond falls below this limit, the penalties are severe and are deducted from the wages of the lathe worker. Whatever the case the lathe worker has to note the initial weight and the final weight of the cleaned diamond and write it on a slip that is despatched to the traders. A worker gets three rupees for cutting and cleaning diamond

The second step is the polishing of the cleaned and shaped diamonds on a rotating polisher. Again the workers check the state of the diamond from time to time by using magnifying glasses. This operation is very delicate since the danger of eroding the diamond shape is always there. The main task in polishing the diamond is shaping the diamond into an octahedron with four faces each on top and below. This structure provides the lustre and sparkle to the diamonds. A skilled worker can polish about 15 small or 12 big *nags* in a shift of eight hours. The wage paid to a polisher is four rupees per piece.

A highly skilled worker may earn even up to Rs. 100 per day. The monthly earnings of a worker from diamond work varied between Rs. 400 to Rs. 3000. Such a variation in the earnings is mainly due to the difference in the skill possessed by the workers and the time they are able to devote to diamond work. The time they can devote depends on the demand for labour for own agricultural work and the availability of family labour to meet the demand. The number of days of employment for a diamond worker among the sample households varied from 90 to 300 days in a year. Many of those involved in diamond work constantly switch employment from agriculture to diamond work and vice versa particularly during peak agricultural season.

Training

In terms of skills required for diamond work, every worker has to first get trained by enrolling as a trainee in a diamond processing centre in the village. Normally, the duration of the training is for three months. A trainee has to pay the owner a fee of Rs. 500 for getting trained in polishing work and Rs. 1500 for cutting work. Deftness and speed are the two crucial requirements to become a skilled diamond worker. Those who pick up the skill would continue and those who fail would discontinue from diamond polishing. For many, the training obtained in the village would serve as a stepping stone to migrate to Surat and Ahmedabad where they can pursue diamond work requiring higher skills.

Migration

As mentioned earlier, members from a significant number of households migrate to places like Ahmedabad, Surat and Limdi. Such migration to cities helps a worker to earn much higher income as compared to working in the village. Diamond polishing work carried out in the cities is of a much higher quality and skill. The wages paid are also much higher. A lathe worker would get about Rs. 10-12 per piece and a polisher would get Rs. 17-18 per piece. For a highly skilled worker there is scope to earn even up to Rs. 10,000 per month from the diamond work though there are high variations among workers in their earnings. Among the migrant workers from the sample households, there was variation in their monthly earnings from Rs. 1,500 to Rs. 10,000.

The diamond work goes on throughout the year. For a migrant, a suitable place to reside while in city becomes important. While some of the migrants have built or bought their own houses; some live in rented houses. Some also live with their relatives who have migrated permanently to these cities for diamond work. The investment by migrants in owning or renting a house in a city has been made possible by the regular income earning prospects of the diamond polishing work. These migrants remit regularly part of their earnings back home. They return to the village regularly for remitting income; to take part in agricultural work; to participate in marriages and festivals and also to rest for a while after a long stretch of work in the city.

The diamond workers both in the village and in cities work on casual basis. Except the wage based on piece rate, they are not entitled to any other allowances. The fear of wage cut or retrenchment in case of a depression in the diamond industry looms large over these workers. As it happened in Surat in 1997 and 2000, because of the recession, the owners of diamond processing units resorted to unannounced wage cuts forcing the workers to go on a strike protesting against the measure. Another risk is the damage that the strenuous nature of this activity causes to the eyes, reducing the period of their employment considerably. If a person is involved in this activity from the age of 15, then by the time he is 35 or 40 the damage would have been done. However, most villagers feel that it is a cost to be borne to earn a reasonable living.

Despite these risks, the diversification into diamond polishing work has been perceived quite positively by the villagers. It has given them an avenue for supplementing substantially the income and employment from agriculture. The risk of rainfed agriculture, as a result, has been reduced considerably.

5. CONCLUSION

The process of occupational diversification as witnessed in the study villages, thus, has many urban facets to its character. The emergence of construction work in the case of Mahudi and Mahunala, and diamond polishing in Bodiya as the dominant form of diversification itself is the direct consequence of the process of both urbanization and industrialization that has taken place in the region. A kind of mutual dependence of the rural and urban livelihood systems could be seen in the process; the urban economy looking for unskilled and cheap labour; and the villages like Mahudi, Mahunala and Bodiya ever ready to supply such labour force. The result is the creation of a large scale demand for casual labour force from these villages and the emergence of rural to urban labour migration in the process. At the same time, the nature of the actual activity pursued has an influence on the nature of migration. Diamond polishing is a skill based activity with a scope for further advancement of earning capacity. Those who are able to pick up the skill in rural areas have been able to migrate to cities even permanently to earn more. Capitalising on the urban links established during migration, some of them are able to emerge as entrepreneurs in rural areas as could be seen in Bodiya.

Unlike in diamond polishing, the employment in the construction activity as available in cities to labourers from Mahudi and Mahunala provides very little scope for any upward mobility both in terms of earnings and skill. Coupled with the complex socio-economic milieu of the Bhil labourers, the labour migration from these villages to cities has assumed a circulatory form. A clear push and pull interplay between rural and urban livelihood systems could be seen in the case of the migration of labourers for construction work.

While occupational diversification with urban linkage has helped in supplementing the rural livelihood in semi-arid areas; a major negative dimension of this diversification as could be seen in the case of both the dominant activities studied is the highly unfavourable terms of employment prevalent for the rural labour force. Besides the employment being highly casual, none of the protective measures enunciated in various labour laws have come to the rescue of the migrant labourers. The highly deplorable living and working conditions under construction activity even leaves it much to be desired as a form of diversification. But despite the negative feature, diversification into activities like diamond polishing and construction work continues relentlessly as not many alternatives are available to households from these semi-arid villages.

6

IMPACT OF DEVELOPMENT INTERVENTION ON DISTRESS MIGRATION

1. INTRODUCTION

The phenomenon of large scale distress labour migration observed in the case of Mahudi and Mahunala has been of a serious concern for researchers and policy makers over the last few decades. The environmental degradation taking place in these tracts has been basically due to the massive deforestation that has deprived the local people of a key means of their livelihood (Shylendra and Thomas 1996). This apart, as identified in Chapter 3 the agricultural cycle in these areas is uncertain and lasts for a short duration. In the absence of alternative employment, labour force, both male and female, is forced to migrate in large scale to potential areas of employment. For most of the households, seasonal migration is a strategy to fight the adversities they confront in securing their livelihood exacerbated by environmental degradation, small-scale rainfed farming and even certain social compulsions. The question of reversing the phenomenon of migration through regeneration of natural resources like, land, water and forest has been the focus of developmental agencies functioning in the region over the last few years (Singh and Gupta 1997). This is because natural resources such as land, water and forests which could be accessed either as common or as private properties play a crucial role in determining the nature of livelihood strategies adopted by the rural households. One of the inferences drawn by the exploratory study carried out in the first phase of the present research project was that to the extent the deterioration in the natural resources base had adverse consequence on the livelihood system, the strategy to reverse the existing pattern of livelihood system has to necessarily begin with the restoration of the resources base (Shylendra and Thomas 1996).

There are arguments that for the success of interventions aimed at livelihood improvement through addressing environmental problem what is required is creation of an appropriate institutional arrangement (Singh 1994). At the theoretical level, one of the approaches advocated to reverse the process of distress migration is to define property rights of the natural resources for the local community with the help of proper institutional arrangements aided by outside intervention (Chopra and Gulati 1997). The argument being that if property rights are well-defined then labour would move towards creation of common assets and an improvement in the environment takes place. This would then lead to decrease in out-migration as the same resources would support higher levels of population. The common property right consists of setting up a structure of rights and obligations in regard to the members of a specific group. The access to the resource in question is restricted only to the members of that group and excludes the outsiders from having any access (*ibid.*).

In the above context, an attempt is made in the present chapter to study the impact of a development intervention made by an NGO, Sadguru Water and Development Foundation (SWDF) on agriculture and seasonal migration in the village Mahudi. Besides trying to understand the nature of intervention and the kind of institution that has emerged for maintaining the common property resource i.e. water in this case, the chapter attempts to examine the proposition that if common property rights of the natural resources are well defined then there exists a possibility of regenerating natural resources and changing the migration pattern.

The methodology adopted for understanding the nature of intervention made by the NGO and its impact involved use of multiple methods of analysis. The data is drawn from the fieldwork carried out in two phases, 1993-94 (Phase I) and 1996-97 (Phase II). The Phase I data consists of the results from a baseline survey of 316 households in Mahudi carried out under the exploratory study as mentioned in Chapter 1. The Phase II data is based on the repeat survey of 45 households conducted in Mahudi to delineate the impact of the intervention using both cross-sectional and inter-temporal analysis. The households for the repeat survey were drawn from two areas in the village; one where the NGO intervention has taken place and another where there was no such intervention. A sample of 22 households in the intervention area and 23 households in non-intervention area were surveyed from among those covered under the exploratory study. Originally a sample of 50 households, 25 each from both the areas, had been drawn for the repeat survey. The qualitative data drawn from participatory rural appraisal methods used in the study have also been made use in carrying out the impact analysis.

The chapter is divided into four sections. Section 1 on introduction deals with the objectives and methodology adopted in the Chapter; Section 2 deals with the nature of the intervention leading to creation of common property rights through the formation of a lift irrigation co-operative society for the households coming under the intervention; and Section 3 deals with the impact brought about by the intervention on the agrarian conditions and the consequent impact on migration pattern of the households. Section 4 attempts to draw conclusions based on the impact assessment.

2. THE INTERVENTION OF SWDF

For regenerating the natural resources and sustaining the livelihood of the tribal people, SWDF has been implementing mainly water harvesting schemes, watershed programmes and afforestation in its area of operation falling in the three contiguous districts of the States of Gujarat, Madhya Pradesh and Rajasthan. SWDF has been implementing small water harvesting schemes since 1976 through the system of lift irrigation and check dams. A need assessment survey carried out by SWDF in the area had shown that water is the most crucial felt need of the people. The survey had also revealed that there is availability of abundant but untapped water resource potential in the area. Based on such an assessment, SWDF decided to give top priority to the programme of utilising the water resources in the area (SWDF 1992). Water has come to be treated as an entry point for intervention in the villages. Till 2000, SWDF has made such intervention in about 350 villages.

In Mahudi, SWDF has made multiple interventions since 1989. The major intervention was made in 1993 by constructing a checkdam across the village river, Machchan at the cost Rs. 9.67 lakh. The building of the checkdam meant that the hitherto unutilised water flowing through the Machchan river could now be utilised more productively. The expected area of irrigation by the intervention was 157 acres covering 40 households. By 1997 the number of households covered rose to 64 which constituted about 12 per cent of the total households in the village. The SWDF apart from building the checkdam also invested another Rs. 9.48 lakh to install a lift irrigation system with a 40 HP pumping capacity and a two kilometres long pipeline. A collective institution of member households was promoted for the operation and maintenance of the irrigation system. The institution created was a lift irrigation co-operative society. This co-operative was registered under the Co-operative Societies Act and all those availing irrigation were to become the members of the Society. The group of persons using the water resource and the nature of their rights and obligations is laid down by this newly emergent institution.

The lift irrigation co-operative society of Mahudi operates through a managing committee consisting of eleven members including two women members. The committee in turn elects one among its members as Chairman. The members are elected for a term of three years. So far, all the members of the committee have been elected by consensus. The lift irrigation society has four paid staff, a secretary, an operator, a distributor and a watchman. The secretary is in charge of overall record keeping; while the operator is responsible for the pumping operations through the lift irrigation. The distributor is responsible for opening the valves at the outlets and for supervising the distribution of water according to the predetermined schedule, as agreed upon by all the users.[1] The watchman aids in these tasks by keeping a watch on the entire system. This mechanism that has evolved ensures that rules are followed. The users being part of the common property institution are to respond rationally exhibiting a greater degree of restraint in the event of water shortage. Suitable methods through consensus are worked out to distribute the available water equitably among the members.

---

1. The operation of the lift irrigation scheme is as follows: Water from the source is lifted to the main distribution chamber situated at the highest location of the command. Since, the further flow to the secondary distribution chamber is through gravity, these are operated on a rotational basis to ensure the required quantum of water to the fields. Of the six chambers, three of them are operated at a time for two days and the remaining three chambers are operated for the next two days when the earlier ones are closed. This way, a two-day rotation is practiced. The operating schedule is worked out in advance by the Secretary after discussing with the members. Prior to the water release, the field channels are to be brought under repair, the responsibility of which rests with the farmer. The charges for the irrigation are based on an hourly basis and the payments are made in advance to the Secretary before the crop season.

3. IMPACT OF THE INTERVENTION

In this section we look at the agrarian changes that have been brought about as a result of the intervention and assess the impact of intervention on seasonal migration in terms of its extent, magnitude and intensity with an emphasis on the female labour. This apart, we also try to have look at other benefits that have accrued to the households as a result of the intervention.

3.1 Agrarian Change

Agriculture is the major source of livelihood for the people in Mahudi, which is carried out with the help of the family labour. Before the intervention, crops were grown only during two seasons; kharif and rabi. Maize, paddy and redgram were the main crops grown during kharif with wheat and chickpea being the rabi crops. The success of the kharif crops depended mainly on monsoon. As the agriculture was rainfed, farmers adopted mainly local varieties of seeds and used chemical fertilisers only in very small quantities.

The intervention through the checkdam has enabled the farmers to raise an additional crop during the summer season. It has also brought about changes in the cropping pattern and cropping intensity. Though maize continues to remain the major crop, the area under maize and wheat has increased substantially after the lift irrigation. The major change in the crop after the lift irrigation has been that of red gram (tuvar), as farmers have stopped cultivating it. Redgram used take more time to mature and was curtailing the area for rabi crops. The changed cropping pattern after the irrigation included maize and paddy in kharif; maize, wheat and chickpea (gram) in rabi; and greengram and groundnut in summer. Apart from these crops a number of households have started growing fruits and vegetables in small plots of land, the most important one being tomato cultivation.

The assured supply of irrigation has brought about changes in the agricultural practices in the form of increased use of chemical fertilisers. The intensification of agriculture has brought about increase in agricultural output. The yields of crops particularly, as reported by farmers, have now more than doubled. In the case wheat grown during rabi season the current yield is 13-15 quintals per acre as against 3-4 quintals per acre obtained before the intervention. Similar kind of yield changes was reported by farmers in the case of other crops like maize and chickpea.

The increase in food production has enabled these farmers to achieve self-sufficiency allowing them to sell their surplus produce in the market. The dependency on the public distribution system (PDS) has totally reduced for these households. The surplus foodgrains and increased cash income has provided a means for many of the farmers to introduce new crops. As mentioned above, a number of households have introduced new crops like tomato and green chillies which require very high investment. Those who have raised tomato crops have also been able to earn extraordinary profits.

At the same time, there is an increase in fodder availability due to increased output and new crops. The farmers no longer need to buy fodder from the market. The lift irrigation also enabled these households to grow a variety of trees like nilgiri, neem, mango, teak and acacia. The SWDF under the agro-forestry scheme has encouraged the farmers to raise small tree plantations on their wastelands and bunds by supplying saplings. The availability of water has enabled good growth of trees. Besides meeting their timber and fuelwood needs, farmers are now able to generate some cash income through sale of trees.

3.2 Impact on Seasonal Migration

Seasonal migration has been an important supplementary source of livelihood for majority of the households

(76 per cent) in Mahudi. In majority of these migrating households, both men and women migrate along with their young children to far-off places. Most of the households migrate both during winter and summer season for sustaining their livelihood.

To examine the impact of the intervention on seasonal migration, we look at the extent and magnitude of migration between households in the intervention and non-intervention area of the village at two points in time, 1993-94 and 1996-97. The comparative details of the seasonal migration are provided in Table 6.1. Though the overall proportion of households migrating in 1996-97 as compared to 1993-94 remains same in both the areas, but a careful look at the other details reveals that there are significant changes in the nature, magnitude and intensity of migration in the intervention area. We find that from the sample, 72.7 per cent of households in the intervention area and 87 per cent in the non-intervention area have reported seasonal migration in 1996-97 which is no doubt similar to the proportion reported in 1993-94 in these two areas. However, it must be mentioned here that by 1993-94 the intervention was already a year old and some positive impact of it on the seasonal migration could be observed in 1993-94 itself. The data collected during the Phase I survey revealed that the proportion of households migrating before intervention was much higher (90 per cent) than what was observed during 1993-94. This apart, in the intervention area the proportion of households migrating during 1993-94 was also slightly lower than the actual as some of the households did not migrate in 1993-94 as they could get involved in construction work of similar checkdams in the nearby villages. While in 1996-97, members from these households could get absorbed on their own farms due to the availability of additional workload as a result of irrigation. Overall, thus, the proportion of households resorting to migration after the intervention has come down significantly as compared to both the earlier period and the area without intervention.

While there has been a marginal increase in the total and average number of persons reporting seasonal migration in the non-intervention area in 1996-97 as compared to 1993-94, it has remained the same in the intervention area. Between 1993-94 and 1996-97, the total number of migrants increased from 53 to 57 in the non-intervention area, it remained the same (31) in the intervention area. As a result, the number of migrants per household went up from 2.65 to 2.71 in the non-intervention area, while it remained the same (1.94) in the intervention area. In terms of gender composition, one can see an increase both in the number of male and female migrants in the non-intervention area. Whereas in the intervention area, one can observe that while the number of male migrants increased during the period of comparison, the number of female migrants came down during the same period. The increase in number of male members migrating in the intervention area was compensated by a decline in the number of female migrants. Overall, the impact of the growth of population, as reflected in the increase in the average household size, on migration seems to have been nullified in the intervention area because of the intervention.

Further, besides the extent of migration, the intensity of migration also differs clearly between the two areas. This is indicated by the difference in the number of days of migration. If we look at the total person days of migration per household for the period 1996-97 (Table 6.1), we find that it is 189 days in the intervention area as compared to 401 days in the non-intervention area. The person days of migration per migrant in the intervention area comes to 98 days as compared to 141 days in the non-intervention area. This shows that the intervention has resulted in significantly lowering the number of days of migration both for the households and for individual migrants in the intervention area.

Table 6.1
Impact of Intervention on Seasonal Migration in Mahudi

Indicators	*Non-intervention Area*		*Intervention Area*	
	1993-94	*1996-97*	*1993-94*	*1996-97*
No. of Sample HHs	23	23	22	22
No. of HHs Reporting Seasonal Migration	20 (87.0%)	20 (87.0%)	16 (72.7%)	16 (72.7%)
HHs with Female Migration	14 (70.0%)	13 (65.0%)	6 (37.5%)	2 (12.5%)
HH size	7	7.8	8.3	8.8
Migrants per HH	2.65	2.71	1.94	1.94
Number of Migrants	53	57	31	31
Male	33	36	24	28
Female	20	21	7	3
Person days of Migration per HH	-	401	-	189
Person days of Migration per Migrant	-	141	-	98
Average Wage Earnings of a Migrating HH (Rs.)	-	25,296	-	15,147
Average Wage Earnings per Migrant (Rs.)	-	8,876	-	7,818

Source: Field Survey conducted in Mahudi Village, 1997 and 1994.
Note: The 1993-94 Survey was done a year after the dam construction. Figures in brackets are percentage to the total in immediate preceding row.
HH: Household.

The reduced intensity of migration for households in the intervention area becomes further clear if we look at the seasonality of migration at the household and at the labour force level (Table 6.2). At the household level we find that in the non-intervention area all the households reported migration for two or three seasons; while in the case of intervention area, the households migrate mostly for one or two seasons. Also the proportion of households reporting migration during all three seasons is much lower in the intervention area as compared to the non-intervention area.

Table 6.2
Seasonal Pattern of Migration in Mahudi (1996-97)

No. of Seasons	*Non-intervention Area*		*Intervention Area*	
	No. of Households	*No. of Households*	*No. of Households*	*No. of Migrants*
One	-	1*	3	6 (1)
Two	12	45 (19)	10	22 (2)
Three	8	11 (2)	3	3
Total	20	57 (21)	16	31 (3)

Source : Field Survey conducted in Mahudi in 1997.
Note : Figures in brackets indicate the number of female migrants.
* The other members of this migrant's household migrate for two seasons.

If we look at the migrants or labour force, we find that 98 per cent of them migrate for two or three seasons in the non-intervention area; while in the case of intervention area the proportion of labour force migrating for two or more seasons is only 77 per cent. The seasonality of migration, thus, also clearly shows that where there is no intervention, the labour force migrates for more number of seasons as compared to the intervention area.

Partly, the impact of intervention is also reflected in the magnitude of earnings from migration, Because of reduced migration, the earnings per household and per migrant is lower in the intervention area as compared to the non-intervention area (Table 6.1). In other words, the extent of dependence on migration for supporting the livelihood is relatively less for the households in the intervention area.

However, the most striking feature of the impact could be seen with regard to female migration. During 1993-94, the migrant population in the intervention area also comprised of a sizeable number of female migrants. In 1996-97 this proportion has got significantly reduced in the intervention area. In the case of non-intervention area, female migration continues to be of significant magnitude with 65 per cent of the households reporting female migration. Further, the proportion of female members in the total migrant population accounts for about 37 per cent in the non-intervention as compared to less than 10 per cent in the intervention area during 1996-97.

The major reason for the drastic decline in the female migration in the intervention area has been due to the increase in the intensity of work on their field as a result of the intervention. The households in the non-intervention area grow crops only during two seasons. There is a long lean period with inadequate food production. It becomes essential even for female members of these households to earn additional income. It is interesting to note the perception of the female members in the intervention area towards migration. They feel that though the workload on the farm has increased, they prefer this increased own farm work to migration where they have to put in hard labour under harsh conditions. They feel now much happier as they get not only sufficient food and good clothes they can even take care of their kith and kin. They do not feel the additional burden as they are working for their family and not for anybody else. They are able to reap the benefits of their own labour unlike working for a contractor in the migrant place.

3.3. Other Changes

There are many other changes of positive nature taking place as a result of the intervention. One such impact that is observed is the changed nature of migration for the households in the intervention area. The intervention has allowed the farmers to grow crops during three seasons instead of two. The assured supply of irrigation and new production methods have helped them to raise output resulting in surplus production which could be sold in the market. As a result, there is now no compulsion for the households to migrate in distress. The continued male migration though on a reduced scale is attributable to two reasons. Despite the increase in the cropping intensity, given the small size of holding, there is surplus labour in most cases. Much of the increased work also is borne by the women as they stay back at home. For employment the male labour force is, therefore, still dependent on migration. Secondly, though there is no compulsion to migrate, migration is also seen as an opportunity to consolidate the family's economic position. One can see the new agricultural prosperity and migration working in tandem towards economic consolidation of the households. This becomes evident when we look at the pattern of utilisation of the income. As discussed in Chapter 3, while for the households in the non-intervention area food is a major item of expenditure; it is no longer so for the households coming under the intervention area. One can notice households in the intervention area investing in production enhancing resources. There is now increased expenditure on chemical fertilizers, seeds, water and on asset building.

Another important impact observed is the increase in the livestock population among the households in the intervention area. The intervention has enabled these households to invest in buying more of both draft and milch animals. This has been made possible by the increased availability of fodder as a result of increased agricultural output. Second, because of the reduced migration it is now possible to invest in livestock as there is family labour available to look after the livestock.

There are many other qualitative changes occurring after the intervention. Some of these changes are also the result of the material changes brought about by the intervention. A group discussion carried out with a few male and female members of the households from the intervention area revealed (Table 6.3) that they are now better housed and better clothed than in the past. Many of the households have either built a new house or renovated their old houses after the intervention. This has been also facilitated by the availability of timber from the trees grown on their fields. The enrolment of children in the school is much better as the women and young children no longer migrate with the male members. Moreover they celebrate their festivals now on a grand scale.

Table 6.3
Impact of the Lift Irrigation on the Livelihood

Area of Impact	*Type of Impact*
Crop Seasons / Crops	Three in the place of two. New crops introduced like groundnut, greengram, soyabean, and papaya.
Output / Income	Higher yield, output and income
Food	More food and less dependence on PDS
Fodder	More in availability
Seasonal Migration	Reduced in Scale
Living Conditions	Better housing, clothing and schooling. Grand festival celebration
Overall	*Thodu shanti chey* (There is little peace)

Source: Based on the PRA exercise carried out with the households in the intervention area.

In fact, one of the members in the group discussion made an apt assessment of all the changes taking place by saying *'thoudu shanti chey'* meaning that there is little peace now for them.

4. CONCLUSION

The impact of the development intervention analysed above on the livelihood in general and seasonal migration in particular thus is of a significant nature. The major impact of the intervention in water harvesting by SWDF through creation of a checkdam and lift irrigation system is the improvement in the capacity of the local resource base. For a community faced with high distress conditions, any positive change in the resource base is bound to reverse the existing conditions of livelihood. The availability of water has brought about dramatic changes. Not only the uncertainty arising out of dependence on rainfall has come down, the households as a result have been able to increase the cropping intensity and also change their cropping pattern. The result is the increased agricultural output, income and employment. The households have not only acquired a greater food security but also have overcome the vulnerability associated with food shortage. The increased agricultural duration and new crops have increased the on-farm employment for the family labour. The overall result is the reduction in the distress migration for the households. Given the short post-intervention period, though the overall magnitude of migration remains more or less same, one can see significant changes in terms of its intensity, nature and the participation of female labour. For the households in the intervention area, the duration of migration both in terms of number of days and seasons is significantly lower as compared to households in non-intervention area. The major impact on migration is the reduction of female migration which is perceived highly positively by the households. After the intervention, the proportion of households with female migration and the number of female labourers migrating show a significant decline in intervention area. The nature of migration also has undergone a change. The migration by the male members of the households is no longer due to distress reasons. The availability of surplus labour and the prospects of earning supplementary income to help in family's economic consolidation are now the main reasons for migration. The changes in the resource base and migration pattern in turn are leading to many other qualitative improvements. The households are now experiencing better housing, better clothing and better schooling for their children which are the much needed pre-conditions for attaining a higher human development.

It must be mentioned here that the successful implementation of the intervention in natural resources observed above has been greatly aided by the creation of a common pool resource institution in the form of a lift irrigation co-operative. The co-operative institution not only has been able to create membership rights but also has defined clear rules for the operation. There is effective maintenance of the structures created as the responsibility for upkeep has been entrusted to the co-operative. The collective decision process is also helping the cooperative to attain both self-sufficiency and sustainable use of scarce water resource. The decision to change the water rates charged to the members from acreage to hourly basis is one example in the above direction. Again, recently the members of the co-operative, conscious of sustaining the quality of their lands in the wake of its intensive use have resolved to keep part of the farm land fallow during summer.

To conclude, appropriate interventions aimed at tapping local resources and aided by proper institutional mechanism are capable of making significant impact on the livelihood conditions of vulnerable communities. The interventions of the above nature thus can change the resource base, end the vulnerable conditions and reverse the trend of distress migration.

7

SUMMARY AND CONCLUSIONS

1. INTRODUCTION

Occupational diversification seems to have become a major survival strategy of rural households in semi-arid areas for overcoming poverty and vulnerability arising out of agricultural uncertainty and backwardness, population pressure and resource degradation. Given its potential for transforming the nature of the economy as well as alleviating rural poverty and unemployment, occupational diversification is normally considered to be a positive developmental phenomenon. From a developmental perspective, diversification is attributed to economic growth and prosperity which enable labour force to diversify to tap the new income and employment opportunities. At the same time, the labour force may be compelled to diversity under duress due to poverty and other distress conditions. The changing occupational structure thus could be influenced simultaneously by forces of development and distress but in varying degree.

Identifying the extent of influence of these two forces has been one of the major challenges of the studies on occupational diversification. While studies focusing on macro dimension of diversification have largely failed to capture the local level dynamics of diversification; micro level studies have failed to capture the links between the local labour processes and the broader socio-economic changes. Hence a need has been felt for studies which can explain the phenomenon both in terms of its local nature and also take a perspective which is derivative of broader social and economic processes. Further, in terms of broad basing the studies on diversification, another dimension that needs to be captured is the relation between diversification and conditions of natural resources. It is argued that distress diversification has a clear link with the changing natural resource base in the rural areas. A clear understanding of such a linkage may help in drawing policy implications necessary for reversing the trend of distress diversification. Coming specifically to seasonal migration, the need felt is to understand the phenomenon separately from the general process of diversification. Seasonal migration has certain peculiar dimensions both in terms of the factors causing it and the nature of its impact on the livelihood.

The major proposition examined in the present study is that the process of diversification as is unfolding in the semi-arid areas is likely to result in the emergence of rural livelihood systems which are dependent to a large extent on the external sources for their sustenance. Depending on the extent and nature of diversification, such a process may have both positive and negative consequences on the livelihood conditions. On the positive side, diversification may ensure livelihood sustainability especially for the poor and may even reduce the pressure on the local resources. The increased earnings from external sources may reduce the tendency to intensively use the local natural resources creating conditions for their sustainable use. Further, the new links established with the outside areas may bring in additional resources and skills into the local economy resulting in the creation of new development opportunities. On the negative side, the local community because of the external exposure may risk losing some of its own cherished identities. The migrating work force may have to put up with harsh working and living conditions resulting in poor quality of life. The growing external dependence might even reduce the interest of the households to invest their human and capital resources in conserving or developing the local resources.

The present study was an attempt to understand the above complex link between the phenomenon of growing occupational diversification and issues concerning the sustainability of rural livelihood systems. More specially, the aim of the study was to capture the nature and magnitude of the process of occupational diversification and growing external dependence of rural households in semi-arid areas in the context of changing natural resource base. At the same time, the study has focused on understanding the factors influencing households to diversify and assess the impact of development interventions particularly in reversing the trend of distress seasonal migration.

The study is an offshoot of a larger collaborative research project called 'Rural Livelihood Systems and Sustainable Natural Resource Management in Semi-arid Areas of India,' carried out at Institute of Rural Management, Anand (IRMA) in two phases during 1994-2000. The study was carried out in three villages in the semi-arid areas of Gujarat. The villages are Mahudi and Mahunala in the Dahod district and Bodiya in the Surendranagar district. These three villages were selected for the larger study because of the nature of external interventions made there. The villages Mahudi and Mahunala are inhabited by the tribal Bhil population and have broadly similar socio-economic conditions. The village Bodiya on other hand is a multi-caste village but falling under semi-arid conditions. The main aim of selecting these three villages falling under two different socio-economic settings was to compare and contrast the livelihood strategies of communities in diverse settings. The village Mahudi which was studied under the first phase of the project was revisited during the second phase with an intention to further build on the insights gained during the first phase. To capture the dimension of rural-urban linkage influencing the nature of diversification, a study of the living and working conditions of the migrants in places of their migration like Ahmedabad, Nadiad, Anand, and Surat was also carried out.

In terms of the framework used, the study has taken a holistic view of livelihood by considering forces operating both on psychic and physical planes having a bearing on the survival, identity, and continuity of the livelihood system. The livelihood framework adopted tries to depict the livelihood system, be that of an individual or a family or a community, in the form of a Nine-Square Mandala encompassing a nine-fold focus ranging from the purely materialistic outer realities like physical resources, skills, socio-economic space and institutions to the non-materialistic inner realities of life, like emotions, orientations and attitudes. Having taken a broader view of the concept of livelihood, a similar approach has been adopted in the study for understanding the concept of livelihood sustainability. The sustainability of a livelihood system has been taken mainly as the ability of the system to cope up with stresses and shocks in order to maintain and enhance its productivity or performance on a long term basis. For this, the system may either draw upon its own resources or establish necessary linkages with the outside systems without affecting in the process the potentiality of the local resources to contribute towards attaining livelihood security and improvement. The definition of livelihood sustainability adopted here provides a consistent framework for integrating various elements of sustainability. The livelihood can be dynamic and be compatible with development to take care of both the current and future needs. Besides, there is a scope for inter-system linkages to overcome the limitations of an isolated system.

The analysis in the study broadly confirms the hypothesis that rural livelihood systems in semi-arid areas are becoming more and more diversified with a growing external dependence of varied nature, magnitude and implications. At the same time, some form of intensification of the local resource use as a consequence of the households' strategy to diversify driven by forces of development and market is also discernible. One such intensification of resource use is the attempt by households to increase cropping intensity by augmenting water resources. While diversification of varied types could be seen among households with different socio-economic background, broadly two major types of diversification emerge from the three villages representing two divergent socio-economic situations. In Mahudi and Mahunala inhabited by the tribal Bhil population, the major form of diversification observed is the seasonal migration of households. In Bodiya, a multi-caste village, despite displaying various forms of diversification across different communities, the dominant pattern is the diversification into diamond polishing by majority of the households both within and outside the village again displaying a strong urban linkage. Many positive and negative consequences of the diversification with growing external linkage could be seen unfolding in the study villages having a bearing on the livelihood sustainability.

2. DIVERSIFICATION IN TRIBAL VILLAGES

Given the similarity in the resource base, Mahudi and Mahunala display broadly a similar pattern of occupational diversification. A major feature noticeable in both the villages is the high level of diversification that has taken place in the structure of occupation. Though agriculture has remained a primary source of livelihood, bulk of the households were found supplementing their agricultural livelihood by diversifying into various non-farm occupations. The major form of diversification observed is the seasonal migration of labour mainly to urban areas in Gujarat. Over three-fourth of the households in both these villages resort to seasonal migration. Besides, about one-fifth of the households were found engaged in various non-farm occupations which are different from the seasonal migration. These are mostly the artisan and service, trade and business and white collar jobs. The households following these non-farm occupations are mostly those who have some traditional artisanal skills or those who are able to obtain a certain level of education necessary for securing a regular job or able to mobilise enough capital to take up self-employment. The households pursuing some of these activities were found to be mainly from the relatively better off section of the local community.

Seasonal migration in Mahudi and Mahunala in the past three decades has become an important source of income and employment to majority of the households. Unlike in the past, the avenues of livelihood for these households are split between their own meagre agricultural base and distance seasonal migration. The intensity of the need for migration is highlighted not only by the fact that over three-fourths of the households in these two villages resort to seasonal migration, in about two-thirds of the migrating households in Mahudi and four-fifth in Mahunala even female members migrate. In terms of labour force, on an average little over two persons migrated from each household. However, the actual number of migrants varied from one to five depending on the availability of surplus labour and the extent of need felt for supplementing the agricultural income. Female members also constituted a significant proportion of the total migrating labour force.

By nature, migration is highly seasonal and cyclical. The migration cycle starts soon after the harvesting of kharif crop and sowing of the rabi crop is over. The migration continues till the onset of the monsoon. Bulk of the households (over 80 per cent) migrates during two seasons, winter and summer. The duration of migration may vary from one to even nine months across households. In terms of actual days of migration, like in Mahunala, the number of days of migration for a male labour varied from 45 to 270 days with an average of 175 days. A female labour migrated for 30 to 270 days with an average of 143 days. Overall, the total person days of migration for a household varied from 30 to 915 days with an average of 374 days.

The places of migration are the prosperous rural and urban areas in central and southern Gujarat. Some of the major urban areas are Ahmedabad, Vadodara, Surat, Nadiad and Ankleshwar. The villages of central and southern Gujarat are the place of destination for those who migrate for agricultural labour work. Many migrate to more than one place during the year. This happens as some of the migrants engage themselves in more than one occupation over different seasons. The kind of activities performed by the migrants are of highly casual and unskilled nature and broadly fall under four types viz. construction work, factory work, transportation and agricultural work. However, majority of them were found engaged mainly in construction work of unskilled nature.

As identified in the study, the continued prevalence of the above type of diversification on a large scale in Mahudi and Mahunala is the result of various socio-economic factors operating in a mutually reinforcing way on the households. The factors which initially triggered off migration not only remain still valid but have been further strengthened by developments occurring subsequently. The factors found influencing are largely of distress nature which have been the result of forces inimical to development. These include factors such as the declining ability of the small scale rainfed agriculture to support the growing needs of the households to meet their demand for food and cash income; growing population pressure and the resultant sub-division of holdings resulting in surplus labour creation, and the depletion of forests depriving the households of an important source of livelihood. Considering the pattern of utilisation of remittances, particularly in areas without major developmental interventions, it becomes clear that ensuring food security, directly or indirectly, becomes the primary purpose of earnings from migration. Among social factors, the custom of paying huge bride price and the compulsion of making regular contributions to *chandlavidhi* have made households to look towards migration as the avenue for mobilising the needed money. Further, the diversification in the form of seasonal migration has been greatly influenced by the continued backwardness of the local economy. Districts like Dahod in which Mahudi and Mahunala are located have remained very backward as compared to other districts in Gujarat in terms of agricultural, industrial and infrastructural development (Hirway 1995). The scope for generation of large scale employment to absorb the growing labour force is very limited in such districts.

Thus, the diversification of the nature and magnitude seen in Mahudi and Mahunala is largely the result of household distressness. Though a section of the households has diversified enabled by developmental factors like education and capital but such section constitute only a small proportion of the total households looking for alternate employment opportunities. More specially, the phenomenon of migration here is explained by the compulsion of securing some assured employment for overcoming risk and vulnerability than by the explanation of rural-urban wage differential. As argued by the conventional theory of migration, rural to urban migration gets determined mainly by the differential wage that exists between the rural and urban areas. However, given the meagre employment opportunities available locally for the labour, the key determinant for migration will be the compelling need to get assured employment irrespective of any wage differential. The prevailing nature of diversification in Mahudi and Mahunala also confirms the argument that seasonal migration under distress conditions is more a matter of survival than an attempt towards maximisation and consolidation. This is borne out by the fact that migration of the type observed in the study is going on for a fairly long period. Any real economic improvement which would have taken place as a result of migration and also other factors should have changed the nature and magnitude of migration itself. In other words, the magnitude of seasonal migration would have definitely come down, if there were to be any real economic consolidation. This is also substantiated by the nature of utilization of the remittances. Only a few households have a scope to consolidate their positions.

3. DIVERSIFICATION IN A CASTE BASED VILLAGE

As compared to Mahudi and Mahunala, in Bodiya which is a multi caste village, the diversification observed is of a different form and nature though some of the underlying factors causing diversification are similar especially for the poorer sections. All sections of households in the village have diversified from their main or traditional occupations; the nature and extent of diversification being determined mainly by their socio-economic status and endowments. Though the caste status in the village corresponds closely with the nature of economic activity pursued, but over the period a number of castes have diversified from their traditional activity and are engaged in various other non-farm activities. One can clearly observe in the process, some influence of the forces of development and modernization in the evolving occupation structure.

Agriculture remains the primary occupation pursued by a majority of the households. Since landholding in the village is unequally distributed, the extent of livelihood support derived from agriculture varies significantly across the households. A significant proportion of (32 per cent) households also depend upon agriculture indirectly by pursuing agricultural labour work. One major form and source of local diversification is the agricultural commercialisation and modernization that has taken place in recent decades. Besides new crops and new technology, the transformation has been facilitated by investments in wells, tractors and modern inputs by the landed and the better off households. Invariably, the major gainers of these changes are the landed communities. Some new lucrative avenues of earnings have also emerged in the process for these households like sale of water and hiring out tractor services. Despite such changes, bulk of the agriculture continues to be plagued by the vagaries of rainfall.

Besides agriculture, one can observe a number of other occupations being pursued in the village by the households. While some of the existing non-farm occupations are traditional, many new or modern occupations also have emerged recently in the village. Broadly, four categories of non-farm occupations may be noticed, viz., artisans, services, trade and business and diamond polishing. These non-farm activities are pursued both by the landed and landless households with variation in the extent of their involvement. Members from a considerable number of households migrate out daily or seasonally to nearby and far-off places for pursuing various non-farm occupations. About 38 per cent of the sample households are resorting to such migration. Taking also those households who have migrated permanently, one can say that external dependence has become prominent even in Bodiya for livelihood sustenance.

The analysis of occupational diversification by socio-economic status reveals that the extent of overall diversification by different household groups shows a clear relationship with the status of the group. Though a major portion of the households in Bodiya have got diversified there is a clear variation in the extent of diversification across different sections. The extent of diversification is higher for the household groups which are in the upper socio-economic strata. Higher the status of the group, higher is the extent of diversification under the group. In terms of various occupations taken up, there are variations in the relationship as the activities pursued are of diverse type requiring varied skills and capabilities.

While different communities in Bodiya have adopted different strategies of diversification, depending upon their socio-economic endowments, one major form of occupational diversification which has touched fairly a large section of the households is the diamond polishing work. A large number of households, accounting for nearly 55 per cent of the total which is next only to agriculture, pursue diamond polishing either as main or as supplementary source of livelihood. In fact, many of the households particularly from the Patel caste have even permanently migrated to bigger cities lured by income and employment opportunities in diamond polishing. Many also migrate temporarily to towns and cities in search of diamond polishing work. A few diamond polishing units have also been opened in the village by the enterprising households providing employment to a large number of local labourers. However both the entrepreneurship and the labour force are found confined largely to upper and middle castes though only recently a few members of other castes have been able to pursue it.

In terms of the causal factors, even in Bodiya, diversification is largely the result of the household need to overcome the risk and uncertainty associated with rainfed agriculture. This becomes clear from the evidence that most households are utilizing the earnings from their diversified sources for meeting various household needs like food, clothing, education and health. For bulk of the households, diversification has become an important avenue for supplementing the livelihood from agriculture and other traditional occupations. However, given the variation in the nature and extent of diversification across different sections, the impact of diversification has been of a varying nature. The well-off households by combining the gains from both the agricultural changes and diversification over the years have been able to really consolidate their livelihood. Better housing, better education and ability to pursue new economic ventures are some of the visible indicators of the economic consolidation that has taken place for these households. For the middle strata, the diversification has brought in mainly some stability in their livelihood to cope up with the uncertain agriculture. The extent of consolidation for households in the middle strata is much less as compared to the well-off households, which is evident from the fact that a significant proportion of small and marginal farmers continue to pursue agricultural labour work.

On the other hand, for households in the lower rungs pursuing labour work or some traditional occupations, the picture is one of struggle for their survival and sustenance. Though they have been helped by increased labour employment due to increased agricultural intensification; as such they have not been able to diversify in a major way like the better-off in the village. Even if they have diversified, it is mostly of the distress types in many cases even repenting over their decision to diversify.

As a result, while the rich have been able to further consolidate their position through diversification, the poor managing only their survival. The picture of diversification that emerges from Bodiya, a multi-caste village, is one of a varied nature leading to further accentuation of the existing socio-economic divide.

4. DIVERSIFICATION AND RURAL-URBAN LINKAGES

The analysis of the nature of occupational diversification that has taken place in semi-arid villages like Mahudi, Mahunala and Bodiya has brought out clearly the existence of a strong urban linkage. Understanding this urban linkage of rural occupational diversification becomes important for assessing the impact of the process of urbanization on rural poverty; for understanding the functioning of the labour markets both in the rural and urban areas, and to know in what way rural labour stand to gain in the process. In other words, some of the broader processes that influence diversification can be captured by analyzing such linkages.

Although the households are diversifying into different activities based both in rural and urban areas, at the same time one can see the dominance of occupations having links with urban areas and labour intensive industries. In the case of Mahudi and Mahunala, an overwhelming proportion of the migrant households pursue construction activity of various kinds. Over the years, the labourers from this region have almost come to specialize in and hence identified as unskilled construction and road workers.

The migration of the construction workers also displays a highly circulatory character. Migrants from this region move constantly from villages to cities and from cities back to their villages making the migration to assume a circulatory form. This pattern of migration has been continuing for the last few decades and has become a permanent feature of the labour force movement prevailing in this region. The findings from the study reveal that a complex set of factors operating at both ends of migration are responsible both for the dominance of the construction work among the migrants from the region as well as their migration assuming a circulatory form.

As revealed by the study, distress condition arising out of the inability to sustain the livelihood with limited local resource base is the major reason pushing the households to migrate to cities. The household distress condition is further compounded by the backwardness of the region which is unable to generate adequate employment opportunities. Given the low level of literacy and skills possessed by them, there is hardly any kind of choice other than getting absorbed in low paid jobs in the unorganised sectors. It is here that the booming construction industry including road building with the potential to absorb unskilled labour force on a large scale has come in handy for these migrants. Despite some mechanization, construction work needs cheap unskilled labour on a large scale to carry out hard manual work at various stages. The somewhat seasonality of work for unskilled workers in the construction industry gives enough flexibility for these households to switch from migration to farm work and vice versa. The construction industry also cannot provide employment to unskilled labour force throughout the year. Nor are there other activities in cities which can absorb such unskilled workers on a large scale.

Moreover, despite the assured employment available in the construction industry, the living and working conditions are found to be quite harsh. The employment is highly casual resulting in adverse terms for the workers. None of the labour laws seem to help them in ensuring fair wages, safe working conditions and minimum amenities for living. The migrants have to put up with highly inhuman living conditions in the cities as they live mostly in open spaces having no protection and basic amenities. The living conditions worsen further when the women and young children accompany the male migrants to cities.

Given the low wages and also the prime intention of carrying back home bulk of the income earned, hardly any migrant can afford to take up a house on rent even for a very modest living. Only a very few migrants working in factories or with building contractors on a more regular basis were found having some accommodation for living. Most migrants have no other option but to lead a life of squalor. This finding clearly explains the reason as to why the cities are getting crowded with slum dwellers. The dismal working and living conditions create a feeling of dejection among the migrants forcing them often to return to the comforts of their villages.

Apart from the harsh working and living conditions, the study could also identify some socio-psychological reasons driving the migrants back to the villages. The Bhils who migrate to cities as casual labourers back home are peasants owning and cultivating their own lands. Having been reduced to mere casual labourers in cities, they possess a strong urge to retain their self-image of being peasants. Any attempt to stay back in the cities will be at the cost of forgoing the peasant identity. Being aware of the fact that life in the cities does not bestow them any identity, the Bhils return to their native villages to actualize their self-image.

In the cities, the Bhils are an object of ridicule for the locals. There is a strong sense of detest towards the city life and an equally strong emotional attachment towards the village. The urge is to live and thrive in the own villages than in cities bereft of any respect and identity. Further, giving up village life permanently to live in cities is socially counter productive for a Bhil. Such a move not only would invite social castigation from the village community but settling down in cities, in the absence of any kinship network would pose problems in finding suitable marriage alliances for their children. A meaningful social life for the Bhils is possible only if they live in the midst of their community than in the social vacuum of cities.

Thus, a combination of factors which fall in both economic and non-economic spheres of livelihood is found to be influencing the phenomenon of return migration of the Bhils. It is an outcome of the existing socio-economic milieu. As long as the milieu continues, the phenomenon is likely to continue in the same form.

The analysis of the rural-urban linkage process in Bodiya presents a picture which is though not as dismal like migration of the Bhil workers but broadly confirming the mutual influence of rural and urban areas in determining the nature of diversification. The emergence of diamond polishing work in Bodiya presents a typical case of an urban based industrial activity reaching rural hinterlands influenced by many socio-economic factors. The spread of diamond polishing in rural areas can be traced to the strong links established with the urban areas by the migrants over the years. Diamond polishing has become a thriving export-oriented industry in the country. Over the years, the industry has spread from Surat to other cities and towns like Ahmedabad, Rajkot, Bhavnagar and Botad in Gujarat. Many of the entrepreneurs in diamond polishing are those who have migrated in the past from villages like Bodiya to escape the severity of droughts. It is these migrant turned entrepreneurs who have encouraged migration of labourers from their villages to cities. Many households from rural areas have migrated permanently to these centres. It is this link which has played a role in the emergence of diamond polishing units even in the villages.

All the entrepreneurs in Bodiya in the past were involved in diamond polishing. They have a close contact or relationship with those in diamond business outside the village. Besides, an over-riding economic reason also has come to influence the spread of diamond processing to rural areas. The diamonds which are processed in villages like Bodiya are of inferior quality. For the units located in cities, processing such lower quality diamonds would be uneconomical given the relatively high labour cost. The availability of cheap labour in rural areas has made it attractive for the diamond traders in cities to encourage diamond polishing in rural areas. The traders have supported with necessary financial assistance, those interested in opening diamond polishing units in the villages. It is here the previous contacts possessed by the rural entrepreneurs have become crucial.

Besides working in the diamond polishing units located in the village, members from quite a number of households in Bodiya migrate to cities like Ahmedabad and Surat. Such a migration to the cities helps them to earn a much higher income as compared to working in the village. The diamonds polished in the cities are of higher quality and fetch three or four times higher wages than in the village. For a highly skilled worker there is scope to earn even up to Rs. 10,000 per month from the diamond work in the cities, though there are high variations in the earnings. These migrants remit regularly part of their earnings back home. Almost all the households who have taken up diamond polishing belong to upper and middle castes in the village. Many migrants to cities have built or bought their own houses. Many live in rented houses or with their relatives who have migrated permanently to the cities. Such an investment in housing by the migrants has been made possible by the relatively secure and higher income earning prospects existing in the diamond polishing work.

The diamond work goes on throughout the year. The diamond workers both in the village and in cities work on a casual basis. Except the wage based on piece rate, they are not entitled to any other allowances. The fear of wage cut or retrenchment in case of a depression in the diamond industry looms large over these workers. Diamond polishing is also highly strenuous to eyes. One can continue in it for a long period only at the risk of damaging the eye-sight. Despite these risks, diversification into diamond polishing work has been perceived quite positively by the villagers. It has given them an avenue for supplementing their income and employment and to reduce the risk of rainfed agriculture. At the same time, it is perceived also as an opportunity to attain mobility by shifting from the drudgeries of agriculture to a non-farm job.

The process of occupational diversification as observed in the study has many urban facets to its character. The emergence of some of the rural diversified occupations is the direct consequence of the process of both urbanization and industrialization. In this emergence, one can observe a kind of mutual dependence of the rural and urban livelihood systems on each other; the urban economy looking for unskilled and cheap labour; and the semi-arid rural areas ever ready to supply such labour force. The result is the emergence of rural to urban labour migration, both permanent and seasonal. The nature of migration in turn is determined by the nature of activity pursued. A skill based activity like diamond polishing provides scope for both increased earnings and even permanent migration to cities. Whereas an unskilled employment in construction work has very little scope for any upward mobility.

Moreover, the type of activity the migrant labourers from semi-arid areas are able to pursue itself is determined by their socio-economic endowments including the outside links they possess. The well-endowed households are able to diversify into activities with relatively better terms and conditions of employment; while the poor diversify into activities with highly adverse conditions. The availability of construction work with all its deplorable conditions for the migrants from Mahudi and Mahunala and the relatively better diamond polishing work in the case of Bodiya as the dominant form of diversification is largely the result of such a difference. In Bodiya, though a semi-arid village, the economic conditions are relatively much better as compared to Mahudi and Mahunala. At the same time, the social advancement as indicated by the educational status is also much higher. The Patels who are the dominant caste group in the village are an upwardly mobile community with close socio-economic links in the urban areas. The result of such difference is the differentiated impact of diversification on the rural livelihood as observed in the study.

5. DIVERSIFICATION AND NATURAL RESOURCES MANAGEMENT

Regarding the implications of occupational diversification for natural resource management, the study revealed that the depletion of natural resources like forests and water has been one of the important contributing factors leading to diversification of the distress kind. The regeneration of natural resources hence not only can lead to improving the local living conditions but also can influence the process of diversification. It is in this context, the question of reversing the phenomenon of distress migration through regeneration of natural resources like, land, water and forest in semi-arid areas has come to attract the policy attention.

An attempt was made in the study to assess the impact of a development intervention made by an NGO on agriculture and seasonal migration in the village Mahudi. The major impact of the intervention in water harvesting by SWDF that could be observed is the improvement in the capacity of the local resource base. For a community faced with high distress conditions, any positive change in the resource base is bound to reverse the existing conditions of livelihood. The availability of water has brought about dramatic changes. Not only the uncertainty arising out of dependence on rainfall has come down, the households as a result have been able to increase the cropping intensity and also change their cropping pattern. The result is the increased agricultural output, income and employment. The households have not only acquired a greater food security but also have overcome the vulnerability associated with food shortage. The increased agricultural intensity and new crops have increased the on-farm employment for the family labour. The overall result is the reduction in the distress migration. The major impact observed is the reduction of female migration which is perceived highly positively by the households. The changes in the resource base and migration pattern in turn are leading to many other qualitative improvements. The households are now experiencing better housing, better clothing and better schooling for their children which are the much needed pre-conditions for attaining a higher human development. The success of the intervention in water resource observed also has been greatly aided by the creation of a common pool resource institution in the form of a lift irrigation co-operative in the village.

Thus, appropriate interventions aided by proper institutional mechanism are capable of making a significant impact on the livelihood conditions of vulnerable communities to reverse the trend of distress migration. The intervention analysed is clearly indicative of the need and the potential that exists for replicating such attempts on a wider scale.

Coming to the impact of growing external dependence and migration on the management of local resources, the study revealed that to some extent increased migration appears to have reduced the pressure of population on land, water and sources of fuelwood. Certainly, in Bodiya, the pressure on local resources is now much lower with a significant proportion of its households having permanently migrated to cities in pursuit of diamond work. Similarly, in Mahudi and Mahunala, a large segment of population moves out during summer easing the pressure of household demand for resources like water and fuelwood. Moreover, in Mahudi and Mahunala, the sustaining of the low external and chemical input agriculture despite increased population has been made possible by the opportunity that exists for supplementing the household income from migration.

However, a possible negative fallout observed is that the common property resources like forests have remained neglected in the process. Though one cannot directly attribute this to increased migration, the importance attached to the forests in the livelihood of the households in Mahudi and Mahunala has declined with the emergence of alternative avenues for supporting the livelihood. This aspect apparently comes out of the fact that a considerable number of households in Mahudi and Mahunala have remained away from the recent attempts made towards regeneration of the forests collectively. That migration has come in the way of many households taking part in such efforts is also substantiated by the evidence available from a neighbouring village of Mahudi (Shylendra 2002). At the same time, going by the interventions made for regeneration of common pool resources like forests and water in the study villages, large scale seasonal migration as such may not become a major hurdle in initiating such interventions. Because the potentiality of such interventions to reduce distress migration itself can become an effective starting point for attracting the community to come together for regenerating the common pool resources.

There are also certain changes taking place in the management of private property like land as a result of diversification. In the case of households which have moved away from agriculture due to migration, as in Bodiya, one can discern a new land management system emerging because of their inability to devote attention to agriculture. Many of the permanent migrants though are retaining their land ownership, have handed over the management of land to the members of their kinship on share or lease basis. The result is the emergence of absentee ownership and also increased concentration of landholding in the village. Similarly, in Mahudi and Mahunala, one can see land augmentation by way of land mortgaging by those who are able to earn surplus income from migration. However, what impact such changes in the management of land can have on the agricultural productivity and investments would need further exploration.

6. DIVERSIFICATION AND SUSTAINABLE RURAL LIVELIHOOD

In order to make an overall assessment of diversification, a broader question that needs to be addressed is in what way occupational diversification is able to contribute towards sustainability of the rural livelihood system? As per the framework adopted in the study, a livelihood system can be considered sustainable when it is able to overcome the stresses in order to maintain and enhance its performance on a long term basis either drawing upon its own resources or through establishing necessary linkages with the outside systems. In order to answer the above question, a clear distinction needs to be made between different types of diversification observed in the study. If we look at diversification and its impact in the study villages, as identified under the theoretical framework, two types of diversification can be seen at work. There is the diversification of the development kind being experienced by the better-off sections. Here diversification has emerged more as an opportunity both to supplement the basic livelihood as well as to consolidate the socio-economic position. For the better-off , diversification has contributed in many ways towards enhancing the ability of their livelihood to withstand stresses of drought and population pressure. There is also an improvement in the livelihood status of these sections aided by diversification. Since in the process no major negative fallout could be seen, diversification can be considered to have contributed towards enhancing livelihood sustainability for them.

The second type is the one where the poor households have been compelled to diversify under distress and unfavourable conditions. The only benefit the poor have gained from such diversification is that they have managed to survive in the absence of any other viable alternative. Unlike in the past when famines and droughts could largely erode livelihoods in the semi-arid areas, calamities of such a nature appear to be on the wane. Even in Mahudi and the surrounding villages, in the latter half of the nineteenth century and in the beginning of the present century drought and famines were a major cause for the large scale perishing and decline of the human and animal population. (Shylendra and Thomas 1996). Diversification now has provided the poor with some cushion to survive whenever agriculture fails as a result of the drought. Though the intensity of migration may increase during a drought year but the livelihood continues as such without any major setback. That apart, there is no any major consolidation or advancement in the livelihood. The fact that distress migration from these villages continues unchecked indicates that diversification has not brought in any major improvements in the living conditions for bulk of the poor. Moreover, there is largely a feeling of dejection among the poor towards the type of diversification they have undergone or that is available to them. Even ensuring the basic survival of livelihood through diversification has been possible for them only by constantly bearing the harsh working and living conditions during migration and by foregoing their own identity and self-respect (Breman, 1990 and Engelshoven 1999). Hence, in no way one could consider such diversification as capable of making their livelihood sustainable holistically.

Certainly, the process of diversification can make positive contributions. To make the poor to gain from it, there is a strong need for policy interventions which can change conditions under which they diversify. Given the complex nature of the phenomenon, especially of seasonal migration, the interventions have to follow a multi-pronged approach. In our view, the problem of seasonal migration has to be addressed at two levels. One, from where it originates, i.e., in the villages and two, at the places of destination, i.e., in the cities and other places of employment for the migrants.

The first and the foremost need is at the village level for interventions which can alleviate the household distress conditions and reverse the tendency for distress migration. Interventions like the one in Mahudi by SWDF aimed at harnessing the local natural resources are worth replicating on a wider scale. Particularly for communities like the Bhils or the Bharwaads for whom the quality of life to a great extent depends upon the condition of the natural resources, interventions like water harvesting, forest regeneration, agro-forestry and watershed management become very crucial. Successful implementation of such interventions can go a long way in bringing about improvements in the living conditions of poor through an increase in the productive capacity of the local resources. The direct consequence of such changes will be the reduction in the magnitude and intensity of distress migration especially of the female labour (Singh and Gupta 1997). The reduction in the female migration can contribute significantly to the long term improvement in the household conditions as the retention of the female labour can enhance greatly the scope for local diversification and children's education (Shylendra, Rani and Patel 2000).

The creation of appropriate institutional mechanisms like the formation of people's institutions for common property resource management becomes also a necessary condition for the successful implementation of any such interventions. Further, when the interventions are taken up on a collective basis like the joint forest management programme in areas of large scale migration, the intervening agencies have to ensure that the poor do not stay away from participation under the compulsion of migration. Extra efforts may have to be made to bring in the migrant households into the fold of collective action so that they do not forgo the benefits because of their exclusion.

Increasing the local employment opportunities can also influence migration. Enhancing the scope of wage employment programmes in areas of high migration, promoting non-farm activities especially for women and encouraging local growth centres are some of the possible initiatives capable of increasing the employment potential. Only such local interventions with potential for employment generation can alleviate distress condition and reduce the need to diversify under compulsion. At the same time, for communities like the Bhils one cannot undermine the significance of even some social reform movements. There are attempts by certain sects like the Bhagat Pant being followed by some section of the households in village Mahudi for eradication of practices like bride-price and alcoholism which impose a high economic burden on the households. The eradication of such practices through social reforms can go a long way in reducing the household economic vulnerability, a major cause for distress migration.

As long as distress migration remains a reality, interventions even in the urban areas for improving the living and working conditions of migrant workers also become important. As revealed by the study, the conditions of migrant workers are quite appalling. Though there are a number of legislations for the protection of the unorganised sector labour but their success has been abysmal (Breman 1996). Even government agencies have clearly acknowledged the problem of high exploitation of labour by the employers in the unorganized sector (Government of India, 2002, p. 156). Under the present scenario of liberalization and economic reforms, we feel that the conditions for labour in the unorganized sector would worsen further. The major need hence is to improve the bargaining capacity of such labour both through legislative and other measures.

There is a need to clearly recognise the scale and pattern of migration of rural labour force in the unorganized sector. Moreover, there has to be effective implementation of legislations like the minimum wages act to provide the much needed protection to the labour force which is completely at the mercy of the employers. Besides making the State machinery more effective in implementing the protection measures, a strong need is also felt for mobilising the migrant and unorganised labour force by the NGOs and labour associations for enhancing their capacity for bargaining. The role of NGOs would be to organise the workers, provide them with all the necessary information and bargain on behalf of the unorganised workers with the employers for what they are eligible to get, be it the minimum wages or the basic amenities. In such mobilization, given the enormity and diversity of the unorganised labour force, it would be worthwhile to focus attention by type of activities like construction and roadwork where one finds a large concentration of distress labour force (Pandya 1993).

To conclude, in order for the poor in the semi-arid rural areas to gain equally from the process of occupational diversification, the better policy strategy would be to improve their local socio-economic conditions and eventually their bargaining capacity. When the poor diversify they must do so with dignity and self respect. Only such type of diversification is capable of ensuring true livelihood security and sustainability.

REFERENCES

Balooni, K. and Katar Singh (1994). *Economics of Farm Forestry: A case study in Shankerpura Village, District Panchamahals, Gujarat,* Working Paper No. 61, Institute of Rural Management, Anand.

Basant, R. and B.L. Kumar (1989). "Rural Non-Agricultural Activities in India: A Review of Empirical Evidence", *Social Scientist,* Vol., 17, No. 1-2, pp. 13-71.

Basant, R. and H. Joshi (1994). "Employment Diversification in an Agriculturally Developed Region: Some Evidence from Rural Kheda, Gujarat", in Visaria and Basant (eds.), *Non-Agricultural Employment in India: Trends and Prospects,* Sage Publications, New Delhi.

Basant, Rakesh (1993). *Diversification of Economic Activities in Rural Gujarat: Key Results of a Field Survey,* Working Paper No. 53, Gujarat Institute of Development Research, Ahemedabad.

Bhalla, S. (1989). "Employment in Indian Agriculture: Retrospect and Prospect", *Social Scientist,* Vol. 17, No. 5-6, pp. 3-21.

Bhalla, S. (1996). "Workforce Restructuring, Wages and Wants: Recent Events, Interpretations and Analysis", *Indian Journal of Labour Economics,* Vol. 39, No. 1, pp. 1-12.

Bharadwaj, K. (1989). *On the Formation of the Labour Market in Rural Asia,* World Employment Programme Research Working Paper 98, International Labour Organisation, Geneva.

Breman, J. (1985). *Of Peasants, Migrants and Paupers – Rural Labour Circulation and Capitalist Production in Western India,* Oxford University Press, Delhi.

Breman, J. (1990). "Even Dogs are Better off: The Ongoing Battle between Capital and Labour in the Cane-Fields of Gujarat", *The Journal of Peasant Studies,* 17(4), pp. 546-608.

Breman, J. (1995). "Informal Sector Reconsidered", *Indian Journal of Labour Economics,* Vol. 38 (3), pp. 411-17.

Breman, J. (1996). *Footloose Labour: Working in India's Informal Economy,* Cambridge University Press, Cambridge.

Chamber, Robert (1997). *Whose Reality Counts? Putting the First Last,* Intermediate Technology Publications, London.

Chambers, Robert (1987). *Sustainable Rural Livelihoods: A Strategy for People, Environment and Development,* Institute of Development Studies (IDS), London.

Chopra, Kanchan and S. C. Gulati (1998). "Environmental Degradation, Property Rights and Population Movements: Hypothesis and Evidence from Rajasthan (India)", *Environment and Development Economics,* 3, pp. 35-57.

Chopra, Kanchan and S.C. Gulati (1997). "Environmental Degradation and Population Movements: The Role of Property Rights", *Environmental and Resource Economics,* 9, pp. 383-408.

Connell, J. *et al.* (1976). *Migration from Rural Areas: The Evidence from Village Studies.* Oxford University Press, Delhi.

Conroy Czech, Sudarshan Iyengar, Viren Lobo and G. Bhaskar Rao (2001). *Household Livelihood and Coping Strategies in Semi-arid India: Adapting to Long-term Changes,* Society for Promotion of Wastelands Development, New Delhi.

Dasgupta, B. and R. Laishley (1975). "Migration from Villages", *Economic and Political Weekly,* Vol. 10, No. 42, pp. 1652-62.

de Haan, Arjan (1997). "Rural Migration and Poverty: Case of India", *IDS Bulletin,* Vol. 28 (2), pp. 35-47.

de Haan, Arjan (2000). "Livelihoods and Poverty: The Role of Migration—A Critical Review of the Migration Literature", *The Journal of Development Studies,* Vol. 36, No. 2, pp. 1-47.

Dev, M. (1994). "Some Aspects of Non-Agricultural Employment in Rural India: Evidence at a Disaggregate level", in Visaria and Basant (eds.), *Non-Agricultural Employment in India: Trends and Prospects,* Sage Publications, New Delhi.

Engelshoven, Miranda (1999). "Diamonds and Patels: A Report on the Diamond Industry of Surat", *Contributions to India Sociology,* Vol. 33 (1 and 2), pp. 353-77.

Government of India (2002) *Economic Survey 2001-2002,* New Delhi: Ministry of Finance.

Gupta, S. K. (1984). "Role of Migration in the Urbanisation Process of Assam", *Social Action,* Vol. 34, No. 1, pp. 67-76.

Harriss, J. R. and M. P. Todaro (1970). "Migration, Unemployment and Development: A Two-Sector Analysis", *American Economic Review,* 60, pp. 126-42.

Hirway, Indira (1995). "Selective Development and Widening Disparities in Gujarat", *Economic and Political Weekly,* Vol. 30 (41-42), pp. 2603-18.

Hoddinott, J. (1994). "A Model of Migration and Remittances Applied to Western Kenya", Oxford Economic Papers, Vol. 46, No. 3, pp. 459-76.

Hogger Ruedi (2000). *Understanding Livelihood Systems as Complex Wholes,* NADEL, Zurich.

Jagannathan, V. and Halder A. (1988). "Case Study of Pavement Dwellers in Calcutta: Occupational, Mobility and Rural-Urban Linkages", *Economic and Political Weekly,* Vol. 23 (49), pp. 2602-05.

Jayaraj (1992). "Determinants of Rural Non-Agricultural Employment: A Village Level Analysis of the Data for Tamilnadu", in S. Subramanian (ed.) *Themes in Development Economics: Essays in Honour of M. Adiseshiah,* Oxford University Press, Delhi.

Jayaraj (1996). *Structural Transformation of the Rural Workforce in Tamilnadu: An Analysis of the Impact of Sociological Factors,* Mimeo, Madras Institute of Development Studies, Madras.

Jodha, N.S. (1990). *Rural Common Property Resources: Growing Crisis,* Gatekeeper Series 24, International Institute for Development, London.

Jodha, N.S. (1995). *Sustainable Development in Fragile Environments: An Operational Framework for Arid and Semi-Arid Mountain Areas,* Centre for Environment Education, Ahmedabad.

Koppel, B. and John Hawkins (1994). "Rural Transformation and the Future of Work in Rural Asia", in Bruce Koppel. *et al.* (eds.), *Development or Deterioration: Work in Rural Asia,* Lynne Rienner Publishers, Boulder.

Koppel, B. *et al.* (eds.) (1994). *Development or Deterioration: Work in Rural Asia,* Lynne Rienner Publishers, Boulder.

Kumar, B. L. (1996). "Changes in the Composition of Rural Labour Force: Some Evidence from a Village Resurvey", *Indian Journal of Labour Economics,* Vol. 39, No. 4, pp. 809-16.

Kundu, A. (1986). "Migration, Urbanisation and Inter-Regional Inequality: Emerging Socio Political Challenge", *Economic and Political Weekly,* Vol., 21, No. 46, pp. 2005-8.

Kuznets, S. (1966). *Economic Growth of Nations: Total Output and Production Structure,* Belknap Press of Harvard University Press, Cambridge.

McGee , T. G. (1971). "Catalysts of Careers? The Role of Cities in Asian Society" in L. Jakobson, and V. Prakash (eds.) *Urbanisation and National Development,* Sage Publication, Beverley Hills.

Neelakantan, M. (1994). "Jawahar Rozgar Yojana: Assessment through Concurrent Evaluation", *Economic and Political Weekly,* Vol. 29 (49), pp. 3091-97.

Oberai, A. S. and H. K. M. Singh (1980). "Migration Flows in Punjab's Green Revolution Belt", *Economic and Political Weekly,* Vo1. 15, No. 13, pp. A-2-12.

Pandya, Vipul (1993). *Construction Labour Union,* Mimeo, DISHA, Ahmedabad.

Pretty, N. Jules (1995). *Regenerating Agriculture: Policies and Practices for Sustainability and Self-Reliance,* Vikas Publications, New Delhi.

Racine, J.L. (1997). 'Roots of Man' in *Peasant Moorings : Village Ties and Mobility Rationales in South India,* Edited by Jean-Luc Racine, Published by French Institute, Pondicherry and Sage Publications, New Delhi.

Rath, Nilakantha (1985). "Garibi Hatao: Can IRDP Do It", *Economic and Political Weekly,* Vol. 20 (2), pp. 238-46.

Scoones, Ian (1998). *Sustainable Rural Livelihoods: A Framework for Analysis,* Working Paper 72, Institute of Development Studies, Brighton.

Sharan, R. and H. Dayal (1996). "Migration and Occupational Changes of A Schedule Caste Community: A Case Study of Ghasis of Ranchi", *Indian Journal of Labour Economics,* Vol. 39, No. 4, pp. 865-72.

Sharma, Suresh (1994). *Tribal Identity and the Modern World,* Sage Publications, New Delhi.

Shylendra, H.S. (2002). "Environmental Rehabilitation and Livelihood Impact—Emerging Trends from Ethiopia and Gujarat", *Economic and Political Weekly,* Vol. 37, No. 31, pp. 3286-3292.

Shylendra, H.S. and P. Thomas (1995). "Non-Farm Employment: Nature, Magnitude and Determinants in a Semi-Arid Village of Western India", *Indian Journal of Agricultural Economics,* Vol. 50, No. 3, pp. 410-16.

Shylendra H. S. and P. Thomas (1996). 'Livelihood in Transition: A Study of Occupational Diversification in Mahudi', in *Rural Livelihood Systems and Sustainable Natural Resource Management in Semi-Arid Areas of India,* Institute of Rural Management, Anand.

Shylendra, H. S. and Uma Rani (2000). *Sustainable Rural Livelihood in the Context of Growing Occupational Diversification and Rural-Urban Linkages,* Mimeo, Institute of Rural Management, Anand.

Shylendra, H.S., Uma Rani and M.R. Patel (2000). *Human Development through 'Micro Trickle Down': Case of a Development Intervention in a Backward Village of Gujarat by SWDF,* Working Paper 136, Institute of Rural Management, Anand.

Singh Katar (1994). *Managing Common Pool Resources: Principles and Case Studies,* Oxford University Press, New Delhi.

Singh Katar and K.K. Gupta (1997). *The Sadguru Model of Community Based Natural Resources Management,* Occasional Publication 14, Institute of Rural Management, Anand.

Stark, O. and D.E. Bloom. (1985). "The New Economics of Labour Migration," *American Economic Review,*Vol. 77, No. 2, pp. 173-75.

Stark, O. and R.E.B. Lucas. (1988). "Migration, Remittances and the Family", *Economic Development and Cultural Change, Vol.* 36, No. 3, pp. 465-81.

Stark, O. (1980). "On the Role of Urban-to-Rural Remittances in Rural Development," *Journal of Development Studies,*Vol. 16, No. 3, pp. 369-74.

Stark, O. (1982). "Research on Rural-to-Urban Migration in Less Developed Countries: The Confusion Frontier and Why We Should Pause to Rethink Afresh", *World Development,* Vol. 10, No. 1, pp. 63-70.

Stark, O. and D. Levari. (1982). "On Migration and Risk in Less Developed Countries," *Economic Development and Cultural Change,* Vol. 31, No. 1, pp. 191-96.

Subramanian, M.P. and Hegde M.R. (1997). "Migrant Workers in Udipi Taluk", *Economic and Political Weekly,* Vol. 32(3), pp. 1953-54.

Sundaram, K. (2001). "Employment and Unemployment Situation in Nineties: Some Results from NSS 55th Round Survey", *Economic and Political Weekly,* Vol. 36 (11), pp. 931-940.

Sundaram, K. (1986). "Rural-Urban Migration: An Economic Model and the Indian Evidence," in M. S. A. Rao (ed.) *Studies in Migration,* Manohar Publications, New Delhi.

Taylor, E. and T.J. Wyatt (1996). "The Shadow Value of Migrant Remittances, Income, Inequality in a Household-Farm Economy", *Journal of Development Studies,* Vol. 32, No. 6, pp. 899-912.

Taylor, E.J. (1986). "Differential Migration, Networks, Information and Risk", in O. Stark (ed.) *Research in Human Capital and Development,* Vol. 4, Migration, Human Capital and Development, JAI Press, Greenwich.

Todaro, M.P. (1969). "A Model of Labour Migration and Urban Unemployment in Less Developed Countries", *American Economic Review,* Vol. 59, No. 1, pp. 138-48.

Unni, J. (1994). "Inter-Regional Variations in Non-Agricultural Employment in Rural India: An Exploratory Analysis", in Visaria and Basant (eds), *Non-Agricultural Employment in India: Trends and Prospects,* Sage Publications, New Delhi.

Unni, J. (1996). "Non-Agricultural Employment and Rural Livelihoods: Macro vis-a-vis Micro View", *Indian Journal of Labour Economics,* Vol. 39, No. 4, pp. 795-807.

Unni, J. (1998). "Non-Agricultural Employment and Poverty in Rural India: A Review of Evidence", *Economic and Political Weekly,* Vol. 33, No. 13, pp. A36-44.

Vaidyanathan, A. (1986). "Labour Use in Rural India: A Study of Spatial and Temporal Variations", *Economic and Political Weekly,* Vol. 21, No. 52, pp. A-130-46.

Vaidyanathan, A. (1997). "Report on the Workshop to Evolve an Agenda of Research on Rural Non-Agricultural Employment", *Indian Journal of Agricultural Economics,* Vol. 52, No. 1, pp. 152-57.

Visaria, P. and Rakesh Basant (1994). *Non-Agricultural Employment in India: Trends and Prospects,* Sage Publications, New Delhi.

Walker S. Thomas and James G. Ryan (1990). *Village and Household Economies in India's Semi-Arid Tropics,* The Johns Hopkins University Press, Baltimore.

INDEX